INVESTIGATING SOURCES

PETER MANTIN

RICHARD PULLEY

Hutchinson

London Sydney Auckland Johannesburg

Hutchinson Education

An imprint of Century Hutchinson Ltd

62–65 Chandos Place, London WC2N 4NW

Century Hutchinson Australia (Pty) Ltd
89–91 Albion Street, Surry Hills, NSW 2010

Century Hutchinson New Zealand Limited
PO Box 40–086, Glenfield, Auckland 10

Century Hutchinson South Africa (Pty) Ltd
PO Box 337, Bergvlei 2012, South Africa

First published 1989

© Peter Mantin and Richard Pulley, 1989

Set in Times and Helvetica

Designed by Heather Richards

Printed and bound in Great Britain by
Scotprint Ltd., Musselburgh

British Library Cataloguing in Publication Data
Mantin, Peter
　Investigating sources. — (Hutchinson
　history series).
　1. Historical sources
　I. Title　II. Pulley, Richard
　907

ISBN 0-09-182339-0

Contents

Introduction 4
   Asking Questions 5

Targets and Marks 6

1 Introducing Source Work
   Questioning Evidence 8
   Who made the evidence? 10
   Facts and Opinions: The attack on Coventry 12
   When was it written 14
   Oral history: Charlie Portingale's Story 16
   What does it tell you? 18

2 Working with Sources
   Ernest Thomas: Soldier at the Front 20
   The art of the past 22
   The Bayeux Tapestry 24
   Christopher Columbus 26
   Children and World War II 30
   Why did dinosaurs disappear? 32
   Swing Riots 34
   After the Swing Riots 36
   Transported to Australia 38
   Aztecs 40
   The Battle of Isandhlwana 43
   Was Hitler Mad? 46
   'Bloody Sunday' 51
   Gleaners 54

3 Looking Back: Revision Section
   Asking Questions 57
   Testing Ideas 59
   Where do we go from here? 60

Index 61

Introduction

The purpose of this book is to introduce you to some of the skills you will need to make use of historical evidence.

The book is divided into two parts. The first section introduces you to the type of questions that can be asked about any piece of evidence from the past. The second section is a selection of practice papers for you to test your progress.

Look at the contents page. You can see the questions that we ask about evidence are really quite simple. So after using this book you will have a better understanding of examination questions and how historians work. This book then can be useful to people starting G.C.S.E. History courses or those just interested in how we find out about the past.

Most history books in schools are about particular periods or people from the past. Some tell the story of great events; others tell stories of people's lives. Often the book will concentrate on a short period of time: the Second World War, England in the time of Elizabeth I. Although such books tell you many things, they don't always make it very clear how they found out what they say or comment on the different types of evidence they used. This book is different. It does not set out to tell you a story, instead it begins to show you how history books are written and what historians do with evidence. It gives you the chance to work things out for yourself. So this is a book about *how we find out about the past* rather than one historian's view of the past.

Some of the material may be new and we hope it will encourage you to find out more. You may already know some of the background to these topics, like World War II. However we have tried to look at things from a slightly different point of view. What, for example, did children think about World War II? (Look at page 30.)

You don't need to work through the book from cover to cover — use it in a number of different ways. Use it in other courses that you do or as a course in itself, with the first part as an introduction to the questions that you need to ask about evidence.

Asking Questions

It may not be easy to make sense of what happened in the past, but it need not be impossible! Indeed, once we have the sources of evidence, three key operations help us to decide how and why the evidence might differ, and what each piece of evidence can tell us about the past.

Who wrote or made the evidence?
What is his or her point of view?
What does he or she know about the subject?
What are the facts, opinions and judgements in the evidence?
Did the author have a particular purpose which might have affected how it was done?

When was it written or made?
Was the person there at the time?
How long after the event was it written down or made?

What is it?
Is it an eye witness account, a newspaper report, a private letter, a photograph, a poster, a cartoon?

We will be looking at these questions in the next four sections. But first try this question. If you can answer each of the questions above in a few sentences, then the rest of this book will be easy!

Question

Find something in the classroom or in your bag: a book, magazine, poster or photograph. Quickly go through the questions above for this article. See how many of them you can answer.

Targets and Marks

Teachers will be able to see that some of the questions in this book have specific targets (e.g. the questions on 'Bloody Sunday' page 53). Some comments on levels of response might be helpful to guide both the teacher and the student.

Any Marks Scheme is really just a guide. Some markers meet after the exam so that their levels will take account of the unexpected answers pupils come up with. We hope that the levels given here will be taken for what they are: namely an attempt to provide a helpful guide which teachers can adapt to their needs, rather than some rigid, definitive assessment framework. They may also be a guide to students to show what is required of them and what they should aim for.

Questions targeted at: Similarity and Difference
Level 1   Either quotes appropriate parts of sources but doesn't demonstrate difference in own words or demonstrates difference but doesn't quote appropriate part of source.
Level 2   Quotes appropriate parts of sources and indicates in own words how they are different.
Level 3   Quotes appropriate parts of sources and develops a full comparison in own words of how they are different.

Questions targeted at: Distinction between Fact and Opinion
Level 1   *Either* 'it's a fact because he says so' *or* 'it must be a fact because only one version or side can be true'.
Level 2   Able to distinguish between fact and opinion, but does not argue a case or provide supporting evidence from sources.
Level 3   Able to distinguish between fact and opinion and argues case/provides supporting evidence from source(s).

Questions targeted at: Corroboration
Level 1   Finds further information from source to check its validity.
Level 2   Suggests other sources which might be of use.
Level 3   Suggests other sources which might be of use and suggests how they might be of use.
Level 4   As above but also points out problems of other sources (e.g. bias, opinion etc).

Targets and Marks

Questions targeted at: Reliability
- **Level 1** Makes a simple statement or provides a prepared 'stock' answer which is not in context.
- **Level 2** Refers to sources in making an assessment, but accepts sources at face value.
- **Level 3** Evaluates the sources in context, but gives a one-sided answer.
- **Level 4** Evaluates sources in a balanced answer.

Questions targeted at: Evaluation of sources and drawing conclusions

- **Level 1** Makes a simple statement unsupported by source.
- **Level 2** Gives a 'stock' answer out of context *or* refers to one source but accepts it at face value.
- **Level 3** Gives a multi-source answer but taken at face value *or* gives a one source answer evaluated.
- **Level 4** Gives a multi-source answer with some evaluation.
- **Level 5** Gives a multi-source answer with detailed evaluation.

Questioning Evidence

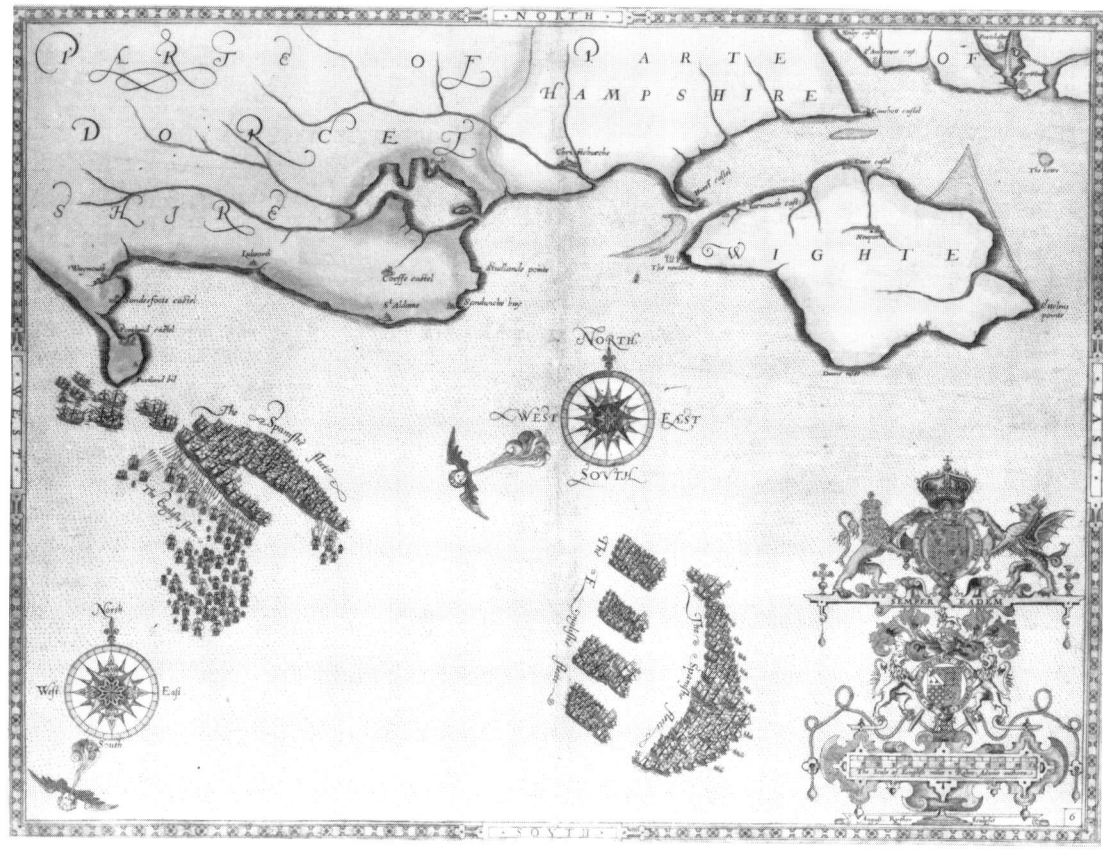

A 16th century English map showing the English and Spanish fleets.

There are two ways in which we can find out about the past:
1 We can read books or watch TV programmes made by people who have studied the past.
2 We can look at what people who were there at the time wrote, photographed, drew or painted.

The ways in which we find out about the past are called *sources of evidence*. Any of these sources may tell us different things about the past, so we need to know what we can learn and what we should be aware of whenever we look at sources of evidence.

Have a look at these examples of writing about a famous event in history, the Spanish Armada.

B According to an English History Textbook

"On the 12th July 1588, the Great Armada set sail from Spain. The huge ships under the Duke of Medina Sidonia were like floating sea-castles. But they were much less dangerous than they looked. England had only thirty vessels of war, but they were very new and efficient. The Spanish fleet consisted of one hundred and thirty vessels which were well manned. There were more Spanish soldiers waiting in the Netherlands under the command of the Duke of Parma. The plan was for the Armada to link up with the forces in the Netherlands. The Spanish ships would then land their armies in England and conquer it for the Spanish king.

The English fleet put out to sea, missed the Spaniards, but turned and hurried them up the Channel. The Armada put into Calais harbour. The English sent fire ships drifting among the fleet, throwing it into confusion and destroying many of the ships. Next day the Armada sailed North. The Spaniards missed Parma who was waiting in the Netherlands with his army. Then a strong wind drove the Spanish ships into confusion up the North Sea.

Storm tossed, the Armada drifted on. Some ships were wrecked off the Shetland Islands. Others struggled on to Ireland only to be wrecked on the coast there. The Armada was a failure. Not a single Spanish sailor landed in this country. Only fifty-three ships of the great fleet got home to Spain. The Armada failed because the English adopted a new method of fighting and the Spanish method was too old fashioned to stand against it."

1: Introducing Source Work

C According to a Spanish History Textbook

"The greatest Armada the world had ever seen was ready. It was called invincible. There were a total of 130 ships, commanded by the Duke of Medina Sidonia, a loyal, proud and wealthy man. 19 000 soldiers, 8 000 sailors and 2 000 oarsmen sailed in that mighty fleet. The Armada was built by a genius and looked like a floating city. 26 000 soldiers from Flanders were due to join up with the fleet.

The Armada set out into the Atlantic, but soon had some dreadful bad luck. A great storm damaged some of the fleet and it had to go to Corunna for repairs. They finally set out and sailed towards the British fleet in perfect formation. When the news that the Armada was arriving reached England, the English were scared and terrified. On the 30 July people in Plymouth finally saw on the horizon that majestic fleet. This sight made the Englishmen panic. The enormous galleons, with their beautiful sails and colourful flags formed up into a crescent, which stretched out for no less than seven miles. The English fleet was much smaller, but its ships were slightly faster than ours.

The English fleet sailed out to attack, but in the first battle we suffered only very slight damage to our ships. The Armada put in to Calais, but this was to prove the beginning of our terrible run of bad luck. The English plotted and during the night sent in some ships which had been set on fire. Our sailors were tricked and our fleet sailed out into the open sea and scattered in the mist and fog. Unfortunately a terrible wind from the south-east beat down the waves. Lightning and thunderbolts lighted up the sky. The hurricane scattered the fleet even more and made the ships crash into one another. Many were smashed against the coastal reefs and sank. When dawn came the fleet was broken up and soon another storm came up. Despite the fact that our sailors acted like heroes, their efforts were not enough to save the Armada. The Duke ordered a retreat, to save what was left of the fleet, but the only way back was through the North Sea and round Scotland. Unfortunately the terrible storms would not stop and the Armada was weakened still further.

The invincible Armada of the Spanish Empire had been beaten for the first time. But it was not beaten by the Englishmen and English ships which it had set out to fight, it was beaten by the weather. Even the bravest of men are no match for the cruel, stormy seas, because it is God and not man who rules the waves. We only lost to the hurricane and the gales, because it was the will of God that this should happen."

From J. Hunt, *English History to Foreign Eyes*, The Historical Association, 1954.

Different points of view can be detected in these pieces of evidence. Besides looking at what they say, see if you can work out how you might decide why they might be different from each other, and what each of the sources of evidence might tell us about what actually happened.

Questions

1. According to source **B**, why was the Armada beaten?

2. Does source **C** agree or disagree with source **B** about why the Armada was beaten? Back up your answer with quotations from both sources.

3. Do sources **B** and **C** agree about anything? Back up your answer with quotations.

4. Why do you think sources **B** and **C** give such different reasons about why the Armada was beaten?

5. Why is it hard (from these sources) to find out why the Armada failed?
   Give reasons for your answer.

6. a Can you find anything in source **C** to back up what is said in source **B**?
   Look carefully for things mentioned in both sources and give as many examples as you can.
   b Do the same for source **C**.

7. What tells you that source **A** was more likely to have been drawn by an English person than by a Spaniard?

8. Suggest two other sources, besides maps, which might help us 'check' what is said in sources **B** and **C**. How might these sources help?

Who made the evidence?

A Contemporary cartoon about factory work.

In their textbooks on the Armada, the two writers retold the events to suit their own country's side. Both accounts may be truthful, but the authors might have left out details which did not seem to make the country they were writing in and supporting look too good. This is a very common problem with evidence. You will find it almost everywhere: not just in history books but in newspapers, on the television and in everyday conversation. People tell you things from *their* point of view — they can't help it, what else can they do? You do it yourself.

Historians must always remember this problem when they look at what people wrote or made.

In this section think about how the job each person does affects the way they see factory life.

Besides the job a person does, there are other things that make their ideas different from other people's. As you work through this section, see if you can work out what they are.

B Evidence given by John Hall to the Parliamentary Commission on Factory Childrens' Labour, 1831–32. John Hall was an overlooker at a mill in Bradford. An overlooker was a foreman in charge of the works and of repairing the machines.

"

'Will you have the goodness to state the present hours of working in your factory?
— Our present hours are from six until seven.
With what intervals for rest and refreshment?
— Half an hour for breakfast and forty minutes for dinner.
Do you believe that the children can endure the labour you have been describing without injury?
— No, I do not.
When your hands have been employed for some time, do you see any alteration in their appearance?

— In the course of a few weeks I see a paleness in their faces, and they grow spiritless and tired.
Have you remarked that cases of deformity are very common in Bradford?
— They are very common. I have the names of, I think, about 200 families I have visited myself that have deformed children, and I have taken particular care not to put down one single case where it might have happened by accident, but only those whom I judge to have been thrown crooked by the practice of piecening....'

C Evidence of William Forster, Manager of Plomton Mill near Knaresborough to the Parliamentary Commission on Factory Children's Labour, 1831–32.

'If the hours of child labour are reduced, mills will be unable to work a full twelve-hour day, reducing the earnings of the adult workers as well as the profits of the mill-owners. The youngest child employed by me is never exhausted by 12 hours labour, which they clearly show by playing and romping when the hours of labour terminate....'

The reason for the differences between the two people quoted in the sources has something to do with the fact that they are looking at the same thing from different points of view.

Just because two stories are different, it doesn't necessarily mean that either of them is 'lying' or is useless to the historian.

To reconstruct the past, historians look at a number of different sources and try to check or 'confirm' what one source says, by looking at another source.

Questions

1 According to source **B**, what was working in a factory like for children? Support your answer with quotations from source **B**.

2 According to source **C** what was working in a factory like for children? Support your answer with quotations from source **C**.

3 What things do sources **B** and **C** disagree about?

4 Suggest reasons why sources **B** and **C** are so different.

5 What other evidence might help you decide what working in a factory was really like for children?

6 Look at source **A**. Does it seem to agree with source **B** or source **C**? Explain your answer.

7 Does source **A** prove that all children were badly treated in factories in the 19th century? Explain your answer carefully.

Facts and Opinions

A Photograph taken in Coventry 16th November 1940

There can be more than one way of looking at the same events. In the section on working in factories we saw that there were completely different points of view about working in a factory because of the very different opinions of each person.

An opinion need not be backed up with facts.

Look at this information about the bombing of Coventry in 1940. Then answer the questions.

B A Broadcast from Berlin radio, November 16 1940.

"'More than 500 planes took part in the greatest attack in the history of aerial warfare. About 500 tons of high explosive bombs and 30,000 incendiary bombs were dropped. In a short time all large and small factories were set on fire. The German air force struck a violent blow in return for the failed British raid on the Nazi Party celebrations in Munich on the night of November 8.

Coventry — the centre of the British aircraft industry — was raided by waves of strong forces of German bombers. The defences were helpless against the vigorous attack of the Luftwaffe. Numerous engine works and large plants of the aircraft accessory industry, as well as other plants of military importance were plastered with bombs, which caused tremendous devastation.'"

COVENTRY

THE bombing of Coventry was as foul a deed as even Hitler has ever ordained.

Clearly his airmen were instructed: "Don't worry if you cannot reach your industrial targets. Bomb and burn the city."

Never mind if you fail to hit factories. Hit houses.

Have no scruples about military objectives. Kill men, kill women, kill children.

Destroy! Destroy! Destroy!

Heil Hitler! Heil bloodshed! Heil pain!

The Orgy

ANTI-AIRCRAFT fire, the Ministry of Home Security's communiqué tells us, hindered accurate bombing of industrial targets.

So the orgy began.

Bombs by the thousand were poured on houses and churches, shops and hotels.

Squadron after squadron dived upon the helpless city.

It was, chortled the Berlin propagandist yesterday afternoon, "the greatest attack in the history of air warfare."

And what has it achieved?

It has proved once again the calm courage of ordinary British people in this hell of Hitler's making.

It has fortified their resolve to fight him, to smash him, to strive and struggle without pause until the Nazi nightmare is nothing more than a sickening memory.

C From the *Daily Herald*, **November 16 1940.**

Questions

1. Draw the table shown below. Use Sources **B** and **C** to complete the table, giving as many examples of facts and opinions as you can. Use a full page.

2. Look at your table. Which of the two sources seems to have most facts?

3. **a** Source **C** makes the bombing of Coventry seem very dramatic. How do the opinions in source **C** help create this impression? Give examples.

   b Do the facts in source **C** also help to make the bombing seem dramatic? Give examples.

4. What impression of the bombing of Coventry is given in source **C**?

5. Why do you think the author of Source **C** wanted to create such a dramatic impression of the bombing of Coventry?

6. Does **A** help you decide whether source **B** or source **C** is more accurate? Explain your answer.

7. Coventry was bombed on 14th November 1940, but some photographs were not allowed to be published until February 1941. Can you explain why? Look for clues in the photograph here.

8. Why do you think sources **B** and **C** are so different?

	FACT	OPINION
Source B		
Source C		

When was it written?

One way of deciding the importance of different sources is to find out how close they were to the event they describe. Historians divide sources into two groups: *primary* and *secondary* sources. A *primary source* is a piece of evidence that came about at the time of the event it describes — in other words, it is the original material. A *secondary source* came into being later — it is often based on some kind of primary evidence.

1. Sort out the following list of sources about the Bombing of Coventry, 1940, into two columns, headed 'primary sources' and 'secondary sources':
   a. Photograph of Coventry taken November 15, 1940.
   b. Computer simulation game 'Battle of Britain'.
   c. Map showing bombed areas of Coventry.
   d. Diary of someone living in Coventry at the time of the raid.
   e. German plan of attack on Coventry, made in 1940.
   f. Book about World War II, published in 1956.
   g. Book about the part played by the Luftwaffe in World War II.
   h. Feature film including the story of the bombing of Coventry.
   i. Newsreel film taken at the time of the raid.
   j. Novel about children in Coventry, written in 1976.
   k. Autobiography of a Luftwaffe pilot involved in the raid.

2. Were any of these sources difficult to put into one of the columns? Explain your answer.

Now read this secondary source about the bombing of Coventry. 'The First Casualty' by Philip Knightley (a book about the history of war reporting).

A From P. Knightley's 'The First Casualty', 1982.

> 'The people could not always take it. In fact the German attack created panic. Thousands fled from the town in an unorganised riot. The army wanted to impose martial law, and an official report described the general mood by repeating what a survivor said: "Coventry is finished". Coventry was actually a legitimate military target, one of the keys to the British war effort, and the German bombers damaged 21 important factories, including the Daimler motor works and the Alvis aero-engine factory. "Here tools and motors were made for British aircraft", the German PK reporter who flew with the Luftwaffe on the attack quite accurately told his readers. The fact that the cathedral was hit and that industrial production in Coventry rose after the attack are two indictments of bombing as a weapon of war. Yet instead Coventry has gone down in history as a monument to German frightfulness.'

Questions

3. Some people would not agree with Philip Knightley. What primary sources might prove him wrong about what he says?

4. What primary sources might the author have used to write this account?

5. Look back at what you found out about the Coventry raid from the primary sources (page 12)). What new things have you found out from this secondary source about the bombing of Coventry?

6. This secondary source (**A**) might be more useful than some of the primary sources in the list on this page for finding out details about the bombing of Coventry. Say which ones and why.

7. Some of the primary sources in the list might not be very useful for finding out about the Coventry raid, but they could be useful for finding out about other things. Choose three and explain your answer.

B Coventry Cathedral after the bombing.

Charlie Portingale's Story

Oral history involves collecting stories about the past, told by people who remember it. These stories are sometimes tape-recorded. The information can be gathered in different ways. Sometimes the person just tells his or her own story. On other occasions the person is asked the same set of questions as other people who are being interviewed about the period or events. Oral history can be used on its own or with other sources.

On this occasion oral history is included alongside a photograph. Source **A** is part of a long oral history interview with a man called Charlie Portingale. See what you can work out from it about Charlie's life as a schoolboy in Bristol in the 1930s.

A Extract from Charlie Portingale's story, as told to the historian, Stephen Humphries in an oral history interview published in 'Hooligans or Rebels', 1987

Being the eldest boy, I was the one that kept the family going. I did a bit of pilfering when I was small, never thinking that it was wrong, I mean in them days you used to. My mother was crying one day an' I said, 'How much money 'ave you got in your purse?' She had four pennies, the old pennies. Well I took that fourpence out an' then it was up to me what I could do about it.

I go out early to Witts, that was a very small bakery then, an' they used to have their vans come in over the weekend where they'd take fresh cakes to their shops an' take the ones that were a day old back — and if you were first there — so I used to be there very early in the morning. And wish everybody, 'Good morning,' as they come in; so you know they seen you, an' they know that you were the first there. Well then for threepence I used to 'ave a great big bag of Burton cream cornets, broken cream slices, Chelsea buns. Then I got my bag of cake waste as they called it, an' then I used to go down to a Mr. Punky; he used to keep the grocery shop. Now on the counter in them days you used to 'ave packets of sample tea on the counter, but you couldn't have the samples unless you bought somethin' in the shop. So I used to stand just round the side of the doorway an' wait for any woman, I'd walk by the side of 'er into the counter so he didn't know whether I belonged to the woman or what, see. Anyway I always made sure that the woman was ahead of me so she can get served before me. Well as soon as he turns his back for the first item she's asked for I would take a handful of the tea bags an' put 'em in my pocket.

Then I'd wander outside and I used to run across the road to a mate called Kenny Adlam. I used to go and knock on his door, and I had a penny left, I used to say to him, 'Now if I give you a ha'penny I want you to go an' get some sugar in a bag for me mum and I want a drop of milk in a bottle.' I got the tea, got me cakes, got me sugar, got me milk, an' I got this ha'penny' so the next place is the railway bank and I put the ha'penny on the line. I used to judge where the train slowed down, because if you put it on where the train did go fast he would flatten it too flat an' you'd 'ave a job to find your penny. But if you could judge where he used to 'ave to stop, always had to stop at the signal because there was a tunnel ahead at Montpelier — we used to mark the sleeper, because I wasn't the only one who used to do it, where he was just slowing down, so it was just enough to run over the ha'penny to flatten it big enough for a penny for the gas. An' I used to take that home and we's got our meal...

Well I don't agree with people stealing things but in them days you didn't think of it as stealing. I mean, to knock the man's biscuits over outside of his shop just because you've been in the shop an' said, 'I want some broken biscuits,' 'I haven't got any.' So you make your own broken biscuits, you go out and hit his stand over, then you'd run off an' half an hour after you get one of your brothers to go in and say, 'Half a pound of broken biscuits' — then we know he's got broken biscuits because you've just broken them see, you're being criminal in a way...

I used to go down Sevier Street near the park, especially in the summer when all the chrysanths and all the flowers were out, I'd take two flowers from each garden, steal them, 'till I had an armful of flowers an' I used to go up on the tip, hide them away, go back home, find anythin', old bootlaces, go back on the tip and bunch them up and go down York Street, Minton Road, an' sell them in the doors and came back with an armful of money. And that was stealing, but to me it wasn't stealing.

I mean because even today if you 'ad a family of kiddies and you were desperate, they were starving, I'd sooner go out and steal a load of groceries and do six months in prison as long as them children's fed. That's how it was then. I'd never get caught, I'd make sure of it. I mean there's many a time we used to sit and have army blankets around us where we was so cold, grate was empty. That's the time when I used to go down the railway bank 'an wait for the train to stop at the usual place and throw abuse at the driver. The only way the driver can get back at you is by throwin' lumps of coal at you, so the more you abused him the more coal you took home. Over Fox Road, used to be a coal yard an' then we used to have Grade 1, Grade 2 things for coal, anthracite an' all this, they used to start separating it. I used to take a sack over on a night time and there used to be one part there with the bars bent where somebody had bent it purposely to get in there, an' I got in there. Been over in the afternoon an' had a look to see which was the grades and memorised it, then take a bag an' get through the hole, fill me bag up.

And I went over one day, I went about ten o'clock at night time an' filled the bag up and I was just going to come out, now this was the only place because the spike railings was nine or ten feet high, just comin' out with the bag when there was a courting couple stood right by the hole, kissin' and cuddlin' and they was cuddlin' 'till about half past twelve from ten o'clock. So my mother, she knows where I've gone, she starts getting hysterical because she thinks I've been caught. I couldn't go 'till they went. But at least we had a fire.

B '**They sit down to the chief meal of the day- boiled fish, dry bread, tea. This is their largest room. Besides this they have two half rooms and a kitchen. They pay 14s 6d (73p) for a week's rent'**

This caption accompanied **B** when it appeared in an article about unemployment, published in the magazine 'Picture Post', 21 January, 1939.

Questions

1 a List the 'crimes' committed by Charlie Portingale in Source **A**.
   b What things did Charlie get from each of the 'crimes'?
2 How could you check Charlie Portingale's story?
3 In what ways is oral history
   a reliable
   b unreliable
   as evidence about the life of Charlie Portingale?
4 What could an historian interested in Bristol find out from Source **A**?
5 Stephen Humphries' book was called 'Hooligans or Rebels'. Do you think that Charlie Portingale was a hooligan or a rebel? Explain your answer.
6 What are the advantages and disadvantages for the oral historian in
   a asking a prepared set of questions,
   b just letting the person tell his or her own story?
7 Look at Source **B**.
   Is it likely that Charlie Portingale lived in a house like this? Explain your answer.
8 The radio set in Source **B** was deliberately removed from the photograph when it was first published. Why might someone want to do this?
9 Source **B** is often used in history books about life in the 1930's. Explain why it might be used so often (give as many reasons as you can).

What does it tell you?

A Representatives of Soviet, British and American Governments at a debate in the United Nations.

The sources of evidence which have survived from the past are not all neatly labelled and packaged. Before we can make sense of these sources we need to know certain things about them. We need to find a way of understanding any source — be it a newspaper, map or even a photograph.

As you look at these photographs try and work out what you think the historian might need to know, so as to make sense of them.

In his book 'Pictures on a Page', Harold Evans explains how the 'meaning' of a photograph can change if you cut or 'crop' it. Source **A** shows a scene from a debate in the United Nations building in New York in 1953. Representatives from the USSR, UK and USA can be seen. The debate was about whether the Indian Government should be allowed to attend talks about ending the Korean War. The Soviet and British Governments agreed that the Indians should be allowed to take part, but the Americans disagreed. On this occasion the Soviets and Britons voted together against the Americans. This didn't usually happen. Britain and America were more often on the same 'side'. So the Soviet representative, Andrei Vishinsky shakes his fist at the American, whilst the Briton slumps forward, fed up, head in hands.

Look what happens if you cut the same picture up and only use part of it — **B** was supplied to the Sunday Times. It can give a very different impression from source **A**. So can the final photograph.

Harold Evans had been Editor of the Sunday Times. He had experience of how newspaper workers cut up photographs. His book was about 'photojournalism'. A newspaper is, of course, just one of a huge number of sources of evidence which might be used by a historian. So we need to know certain things about this or any other source before we can understand more completely what it means.

1: Introducing Source Work

B Part of the same photograph.

C Another part of the same photograph.

Questions

1. Compare **A** and **B**.
   a. What important differences do you notice?
   b. How might these differences change our understanding of what was happening at the UN Debate?

2. What does **C** show and how might this affect our understanding of what was happening at the UN Debate?

3. Read the background information. It tells you more about the debate.
   a. Write a caption to go with source **A** and one to go with source **B**. Remember that your captions should give different impressions of what was happening.
   b. Write two captions to go with **C**. They should describe what is happening in the photograph, but give opposite impressions.

4. What do you think is meant by the statement 'the camera never lies'? Do you agree with it? Explain your answer and support it with evidence from these sources.

5. What sort of information do we need to have to help us understand what sources mean? What do we need to know about a source and how will this help us? Use these photographs — or any other source — to back up your answer.

Soldier at the Front

All you have to do in this exercise is to work out what these different types of evidence can tell us about a soldier who fought in the First World War (1914–1918).

A Letter from Private E. Thomas to his parents in Oxford. The original letter was handwritten.

> Private E. Thomas 2584,
> C Company 11 Platoon,
> 1/4 Oxon. & Bucks Lt. Infty.
> British Expeditionary Force.
> France.
>
> Monday, Nov. 1, 1915
>
> My Dearest Father and Mother,
>
> You can picture me Sunday afternoon, sitting on the floor of our dug-out in the mud, not having washed or shaved or taken off my clothes, boots or puttees for five days. We have plenty of company with rats and mice; they run all over us day and night, and what would you say if I told you a decent fellow was having his dinner when a mouse ran over the table (i.e. floor), he struck and hit it on the end of his fork then he threw it outside, wiped his fork on his trousers and went on with grub as if nothing had taken place. In fact it's appalling that such a civilized nation should be flung into a barbarous war, only within a few miles of the centre of civilization, and man should adapt himself to such games. Like worms, we never see daylight, living underground, and for eight days we only see the sides of a trench, and we eat our food with hands and live and sleep in dirty little caves; it seems a shocking way of going on. Our chief occupation is making cocoa, which we do all day and night, but alas if the Allemands spot some smoke over come some grenades and shells and up goes the apple cart; of course we don't forget to return the compliment. You warn me of snipers. We are 200 yards from the Germans, so snipers are not much use, only when the trenches run close, such as 30 yards or so, but when they are farther apart there is a greater danger that is shell fire. They cannot shell us when they are only 40 yards apart, for fear of hitting their own men, but we are 200, so get beaucoup shells etc. Last night whilst clinging(?) on the parapet when I dug up a dead German, talk about fish paste, but we get used to this sort of thing and think no more of this than looking at a dead cow.

C Ernest Thomas in uniform of 2nd Lieutenant, 1917

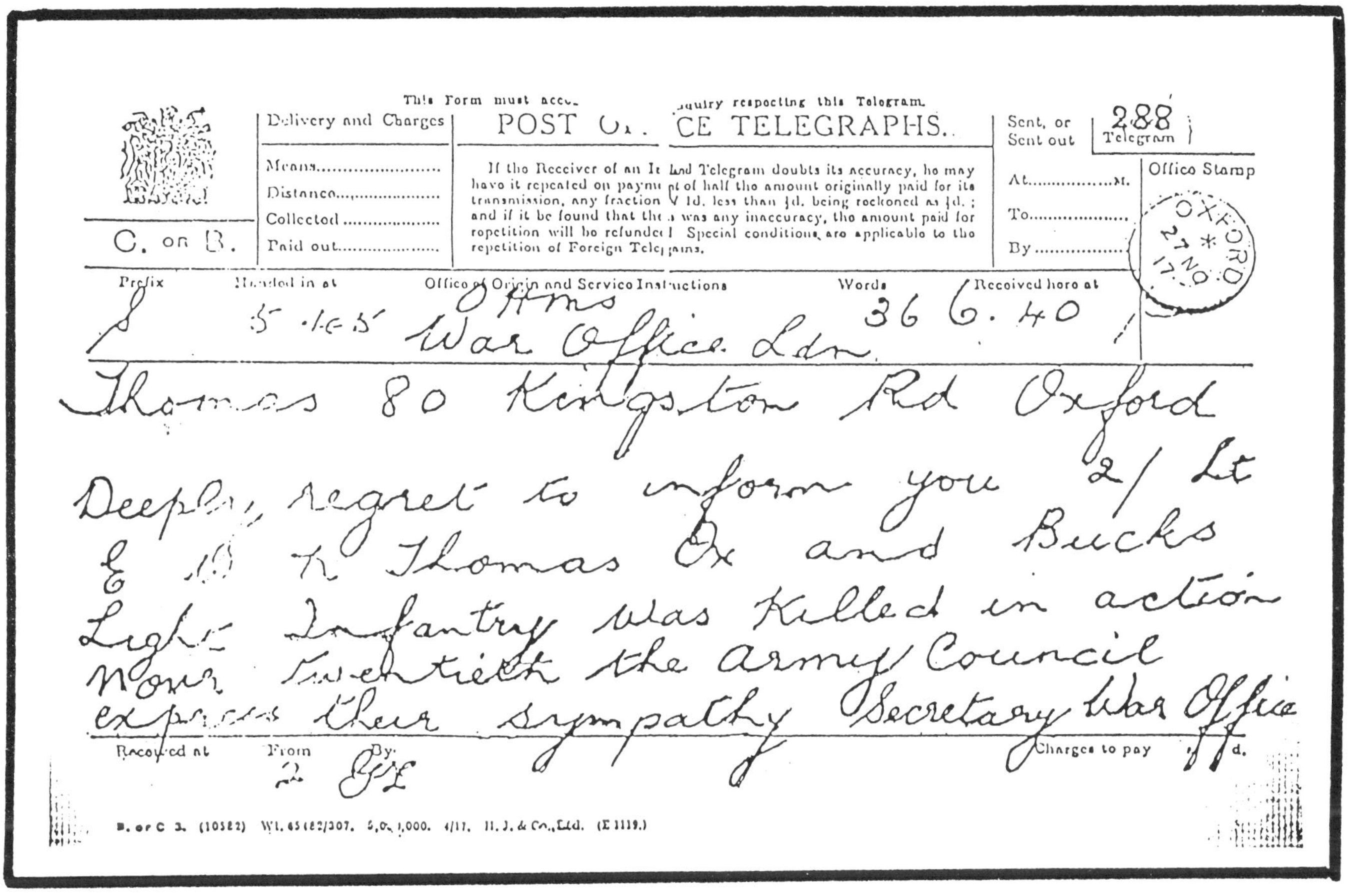

This Form must acc... ...quiry respecting this Telegram.

POST O... CE TELEGRAPHS.

Delivery and Charges: Means........ Distance........ Collected........ Paid out........

C. or B.

If the Receiver of an In... Land Telegram doubts its accuracy, he may have it repeated on paym...nt of half the amount originally paid for its transmission, any fraction of 1d. less than ½d. being reckoned as ½d.; and if it be found that the... was any inaccuracy, the amount paid for repetition will be refunded. Special conditions are applicable to the repetition of Foreign Telegrams.

Sent, or Sent out: 288 Telegram

At........M. To........ By........

Office Stamp: OXFORD 27 NO 17

Prefix: S | Handed in at: 5.45 | Office of Origin and Service Instructions: OHMS War Office Ldn | Words: 36 | Received here at: 6.40

Thomas 80 Kingston Rd Oxford

Deeply regret to inform you 2/Lt E W K Thomas Ox and Bucks Light Infantry was killed in action Nov twentieth the Army Council express their sympathy Secretary War Office

Received at | From: 2 | By: GL | Charges to pay ... d.

B. or C. 3. (10582) Wt. 65182/307. 5,0..,000. 4/17. H. J. & Co., Ltd. (E 1119.)

B **Telegram from the War Office**

Questions

1 When was document **B** sent and what does it say?

2 How do we know that document **B** is an official document?

3 When was document **A** written?

4 What details does document **A** give us about life in the trenches? Write out parts of the evidence to help you.

5 Look at **C**. What can we find out about Ernest Thomas from this photograph?

6 Which of the three documents is most useful to a historian trying to find out about
a The First World War
b Ernest Thomas
c The Post Office
Give reasons for each answer.

The art of the past

Questions

1. What did these Early People paint and draw? (Make a list of all the things they painted.)

2. What can we learn about Early People from looking at their paintings?
   Which of the following sentences about Early People's lives can we prove from their paintings? Copy each sentence. Write TRUE or FALSE alongside each sentence. Explain your answer carefully.
   a Early People hunted animals.
   b Early People hunted animals alone.
   c Sometimes traps were made for animals.
   d Sometimes weapons were used to hunt animals.
   e The paintings give us a good idea what Early People looked like.
   f The paintings tell us much about the homes of Early People.
   g Early People were able to hunt animals larger and stronger than themselves.
   h Early People were able to hunt animals that were faster than themselves.
   i Early People were always successful hunters.
   j Early People grew food to eat.
   k Early People knew something about the insides of animals.

3. Sometimes it is difficult to be certain which animal Early People painted. (Write down or draw one example of a painting where you couldn't be sure — try and name the animals it could be.)

4. Choose two sources and write about:
   a What similarities you notice.
   b What differences you notice.

5. These sources were made by people who lived far away and at a different times from each other. What did these people have in common?

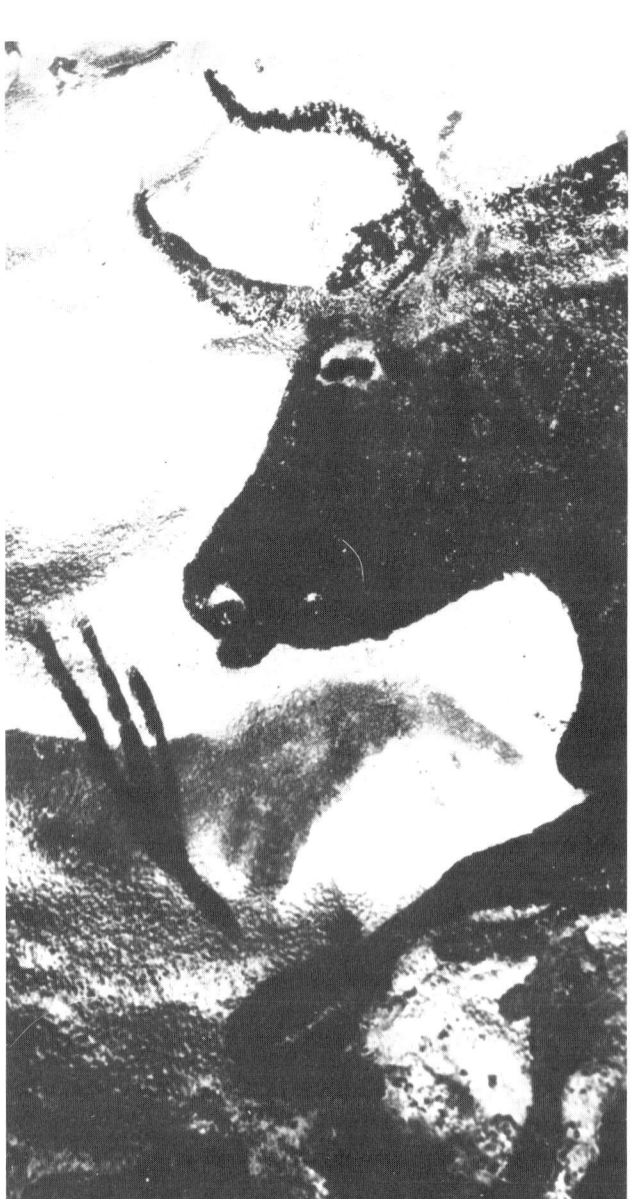

A Copy of a rock painting 15000–10000 BC from Lascaux, Southern France

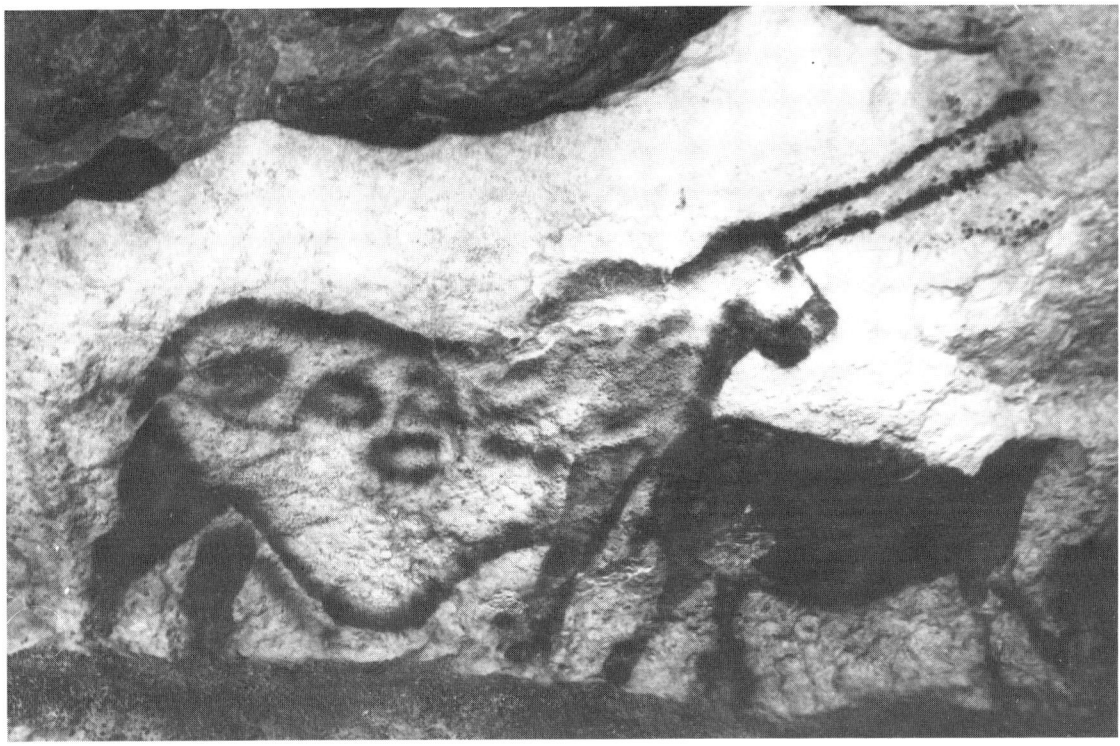

B Copy of a rock painting 1500–10000 BC from Lascaux, Southern France

C Rock painting, about 3000 BC, Algeria, North Africa

The Bayeux Tapestry

There are many different sorts of evidence and this evidence can tell us different things. These things might not have been intended as the original main idea or message in the source, but they can be useful for historians; they can give us valuable clues about the people who made the evidence and about the times in which they live.

One famous example of this is the Bayeux Tapestry. Actually it's not a tapestry, it is an embroidery. Many people know it because it tells a story of the events of 1066. In fact, the Tapestry tells us a longer story and starts in 1064. Some of the most famous scenes in the Tapestry are about the Battle of Hastings, but if we look at it more carefully we can find out about a number of things besides the battle.

To answer these questions you will need to look very carefully at the pictures. Support your answers by mentioning as many detailed examples as you can. You may also like to include sketches.

A   **Panel from the Bayeux Tapestry**

B Panel from the Bayeux Tapestry

Questions

1 Look at Sources **A** and **B**.
  What do these scenes from the Tapestry tell us about:
  a clothing
  b farming
  c writing
  d food and its preparation
  e how food was eaten

2 'Only famous people were shown in the Tapestry.' Do these sources show this statement to be true? Explain your answer.

3 What sources of evidence could we use to check if the Tapestry is reliable evidence about any of the things mentioned in question 1? How would they help?

4 The people and things shown in the Tapestry look more like cartoon characters than realistic pictures. Does this mean that we can't rely on the Tapestry as evidence about the things mentioned in question 1? Explain your answer.

Christopher Columbus

When you look at a document it is easy to believe everything it says. For example, a lot of people believe that everything they read in the newspapers is the truth. Stories seem to make sense, so there is often no reason to suppose that there might be a problem. The newspapers and TV just tell us what happened. But do they? When we read other accounts of the same event we often find that they don't completely agree with one another.

Comparing accounts of the same event can raise questions about all sorts of details.

Documents from the past raise even more questions, especially when we are looking at people or events that were not recorded in great detail. Even quite famous things weren't always written down in a very accurate way.

The example we are going to look at is the story of Christopher Columbus. This story is so famous that it might seem to be easy to find the truth about. After all, everybody seems to know that Columbus was the first European to reach the Americas, but what else do we know about him? What details do we know about the voyage? What sources of evidence might we use to find out about things that happened 400 years ago? Can we trust what we read in books about the past?

B **Map of the first voyage of Columbus, included in 'The Widening World'**

Many of us first heard about Christopher Columbus in school, so what do schoolbooks say about him? In this exercise we will examine what two different schoolbooks said.

A **From 'The Widening World', a school textbook about English history, published in 1954 by George Philip & Son Ltd [One of its 42 short chapters (each of 5–6 pages) is about Christopher Columbus].**

66

Christopher Columbus was born in Genoa. His father had a little wine-shop where men came and talked.

Columbus went to live in Lisbon, the great port of Portugal. From there he went on several long voyages, on which he learnt a great deal about ships and tides and winds. He talked with men who made maps, and he read books. Gradually he came to agree with those men who were convinced that the world was round, and that if he sailed west long enough he would reach Japan, China and India. It was a bold plan — to sail west to get to the East.

For seven years he tried to persuade rich men to help him, but they laughed at his ideas. At last, in 1492, Queen Isabel of Spain helped him. Joyfully he went down to the sea and obtained three ships, the *Santa Maria*, the *Nina*, and the *Pinta*. A hundred and twenty men set sail with him. Each day, each hour, the men hoped to see land. But they could see only the sea.

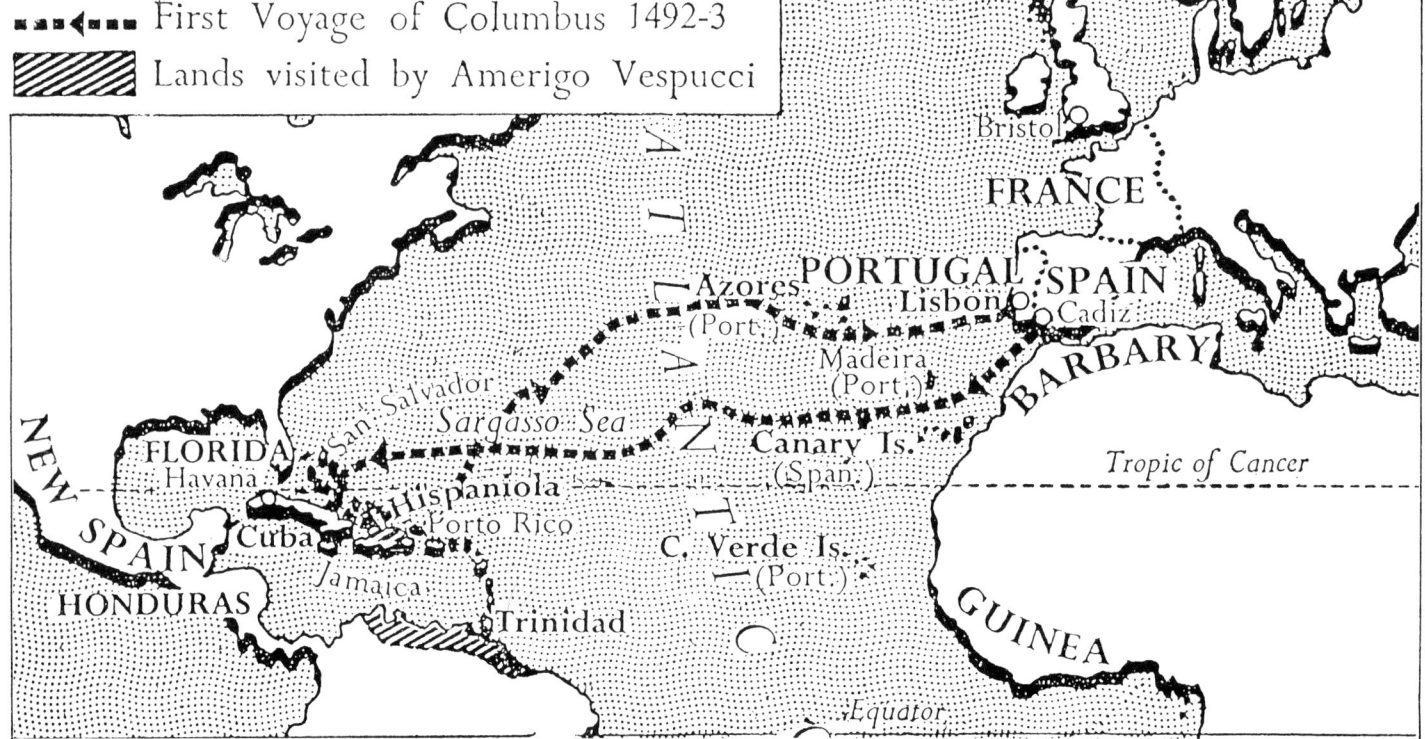

They began to hate Columbus, and even plotted to kill him. Columbus told them that they would soon see land, but even he was worried. Then suddenly they thought that he was right. A great brown mass stretched ahead of them, as far as they could see. But it was not land. It was seaweed!

At last, one night, a light was seen by those who were watching. In the morning Columbus and his men found that they were approaching the shores of a beautifully wooded island. After sailing for thirty days they had found a new land.

Columbus was sure that the islands he had discovered were very near to India and China, and so he named them the 'West Indies', and even today that is their name. You can look at your map and see how wrong Columbus was in thinking that these islands were near to India and China.

C Extracts from 'Christopher Columbus' by L du Garde Peach, published by Ladybird in 1961. All of its 50 pages describe Columbus' first voyage.

When Christopher Columbus sailed from the little port of Palos, in Spain, on August the third, in the year 1492, he commenced a voyage which changed the course of history.

Christopher Columbus was born in Genoa, in Italy, between the years 1440 and 1450, although the exact date is not known.

We know very little about the early life of Columbus. His father was a weaver, and for a time Christopher certainly worked in the family business.

Columbus knew, or at least believed that the earth was round. Nobody knew this for certain, because no one had ever travelled right round it; but Columbus thought that by sailing straight to the west he would come to Japan, which other explorers had reached by journeying across land and sea to the east.

Believing that there was no hope of help in Spain, Columbus set out to join his brother in France. On the way he rested at a monastery near Palos . . . At this monastery there was a friar named Juan Perez, who had been chaplain to the Queen of Spain. He had faith in Columbus and agreed to write to the Queen and ask for her help.

In Palos he (Columbus) had made the acquaintance of two brothers, sea captains, and what was more important, the owners of ships. Their names were Martin Alonso Pinzon and Vicente Yañez Pinzon.

D Map of the first voyage of Columbus included in the Ladybird book

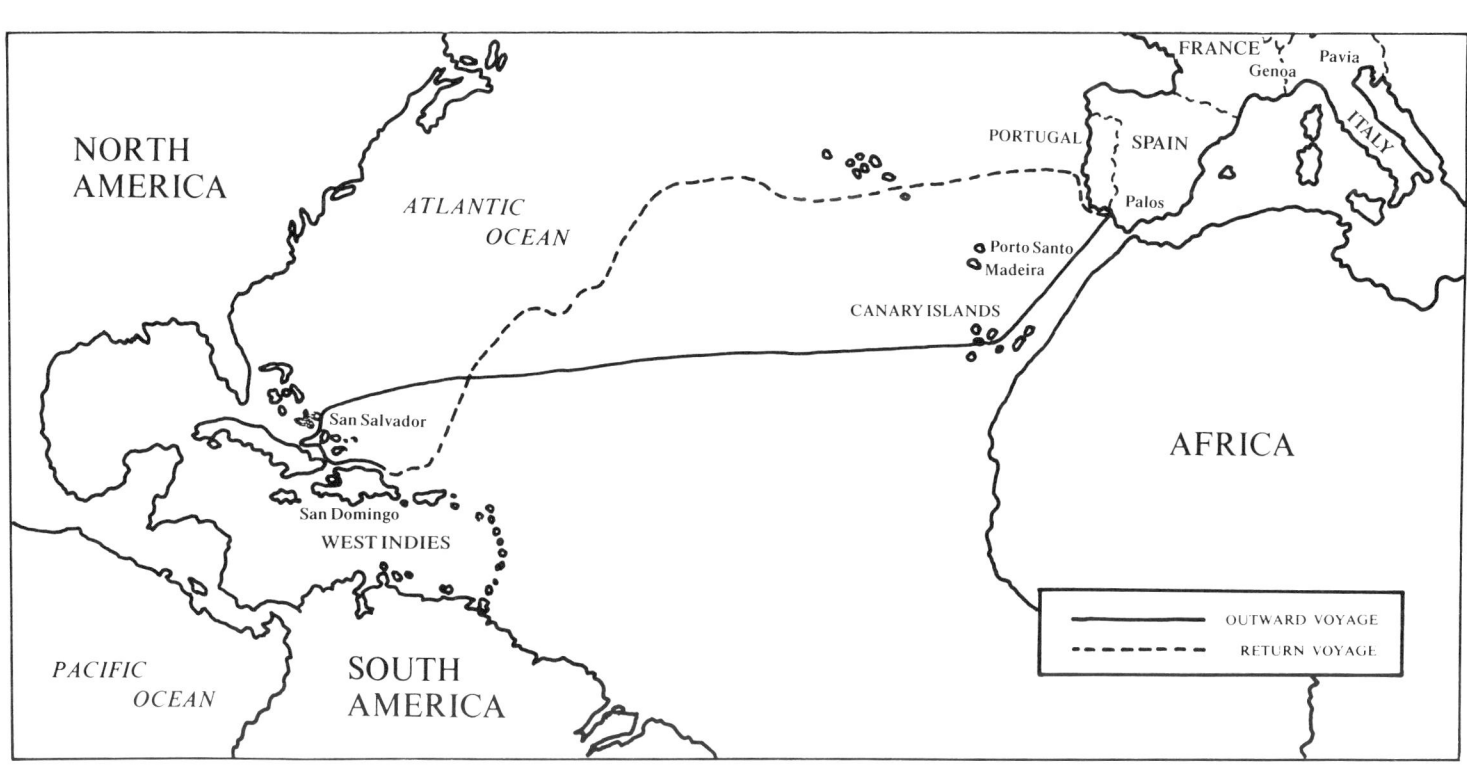

Christopher Columbus

With their help he finally obtained three small ships. Their names were 'Santa Maria', the largest of the three, 'Pinta', and 'Niña'.

Even so, it was not easy to get together the crews, about 90 men in all, necessary to man the three ships...

The sailors were satisfied for the moment. But they continued to express their fears amongst themselves until some of them were ready to mutiny. They wanted to throw Columbus overboard and sail back to Spain.

Then, one evening, one of the sailors called out that he had sighted land... All night they waited anxiously for the dawn, but when the morning came, the land was not there. What the sailor had seen was a low-lying cloud.

Then from a sailor high up at the masthead of the 'Niña' came the cry, 'Land ho!'

It was land at last! The long weeks, with nothing but sea all about them, were over. Many of the sailors thought they would never see land again, and all except Columbus were anxious and afraid...

Columbus had believed that by sailing west he would reach India, the land route to which was closed by the Turks. He thought that the islands which he had found were somewhere near India, and the reason why they are still called the West Indies is owing to the mistake made by Columbus, almost five hundred years ago.

"

E Picture of Christopher Columbus included in the Ladybird book. All the pictures in the Ladybird book were drawn especially for the book.

Questions

1 Look at the evidence on these two pages. Then copy and complete this chart.

Source	Widening World	Ladybird Book
a When was Columbus born?	(see **B**)	
b Where was he born?		
c What was his father's job?		
d Where did he set sail from?	(see map **C**)	(map **F**)
e Which ships did he take with him?		
f Who helped him?		
g How many men set sail with Columbus?		
h At first the sailor thought he saw land. What did he really see?		
i What did he call the place he arrived at?		

2 a Choose two things the books agree on and suggest reasons why they agree.
   b Choose two things the books disagree on and suggest reasons why they disagree.

3 How might we find out more about Columbus and check these stories?

4 Why do you think we know more about Columbus' life after 1492 than before 1492?

5 Can we trust what we read in schoolbooks? Explain your answer.

Children and World War II

Most history is written by adults for adults. The sources on these pages are different. They were all written by children during the Second World War. So they give us a different view of the war from that which we read about in history books. When you look at this chapter, think about:

a What things seem to have been important to children during the war?
b Why were these things important to the children?
c How might children's views be different from the views of adults?
d How might they be useful to historians looking back on the war?

D

'There never ought to be wars if we were governed properly. There's always old people in power and the young people are called up and expected to give their lives when they've messed things up. No wonder every generation of young people grow up more restless. I've been to so many different schools since the war's been on that I can't settle down, and then I'm blamed because I don't work well. It's a terrible thing war, such a waste of life and energy, and my opinion is that the country will suffer for years and years.'

Doris, aged 13.

A *Vera, aged 8.*

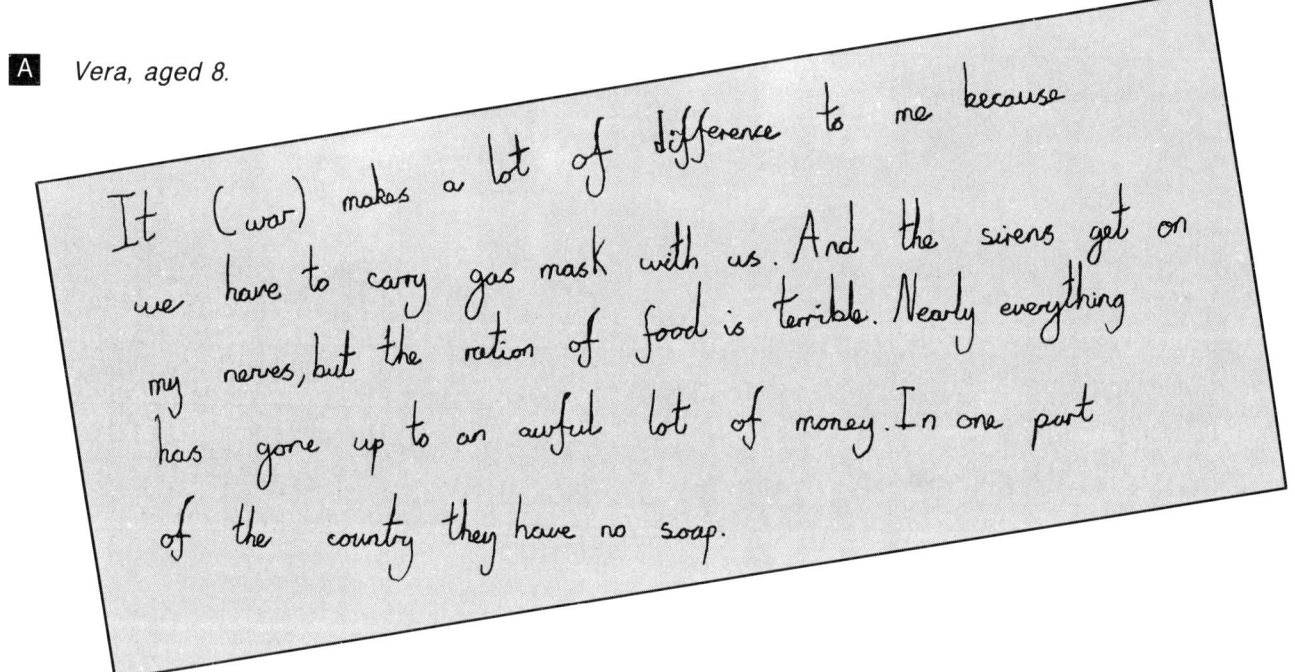

It (war) makes a lot of difference to me because we have to carry gas mask with us. And the sirens get on my nerves, but the ration of food is terrible. Nearly everything has gone up to an awful lot of money. In one part of the country they have no soap.

B

'There's one bit of the war that does interest me. I don't like the way they send out pigs in front of the men. It's not fair on the pigs. It's our country not the pigs. We should fight out own battles.'

Robert, aged 13.

C

'I'm mad on the Air Force. I know all the different types of aeroplanes. I've got a book at home my dad bought and it's got pictures of all the aeroplanes and I know how much each one uses. I'd like to bring a lot of Nazi planes down, and I will when I'm big.'

Dick, aged 10.

E

'I do not like to write about the war because it is not for girls. There are a lot of men that will be killed.'

Alice, aged 10.

F

'War's a damned nuisance; you can't get sweets, everything's on coupons.'

Michael, aged 10.

G *Brian, age 8.*

> The wemen hak to go to war work to help win the war, They make guns and airiplanes to and the men they go to the front to shoot the Germans The schoalls hak to have airraid shelters.

H *John, aged 9.*

> The war is terrible men being killed, and people losing their land and homes and Hitler starving them. Hitler is too jealous of other countries because his own land isn't so rich. He wants more land so that he could turn around to the German people and say "see what a great man I am and see what I've done for you!"

Questions

1. **a** What does Vera, document **A**, say about rationing?
   b Can you explain why she might say this?

2. Look at all the documents. What things do the children least like about the war? Copy out bits and name the writer of the extracts you use in your answer.

3. What is the average age of the writers?

4. Not all the extracts are accurate about the details of the Second World War, document **B** for example. What has Robert got wrong? Can you explain why?

5. Do any of the writers disagree about anything? Explain your answer carefully.

6. From the documents, how did children living during the Second World War feel about growing up during this period?

7. How useful will these documents be to the following people? Explain your answers.
   a a historian interested in the Blitz.
   b a historian interested in the history of education.
   c a historian interested in rationing in the Second World War.

8. Do you think adults in the Armed Forces during the Second World War would be interested in the same things as the children? Explain your answer.

Why did dinosaurs disappear?

A *theory* is a way of explaining why something happened.

In this section there are a number of theories about why the dinosaurs died out. Think about:
a Why there are so many theories.
b How we could go about proving these theories.
c Why it might be difficult to be certain about any one theory.

A Why did dinosaurs disappear? from 'Spotters Guide: Dinosaurs' published by Usborne Publishing Ltd, 1987

"

The first theory is that there was some sort of cosmic event — for example, the explosion of a star close to our solar system. This would have bathed the earth in deadly radiation. Animals on land would either have been killed by it or been so badly damaged that they could not give birth to live young afterwards.

Although the water would have shielded sea animals from much of the radiation, the surface layers containing plankton would have been badly affected. Life in the sea is very dependent on the plankton layers. If the plankton is killed, the chain of life in the sea is disrupted. Prehistoric fish fed on plankton and most of the large sea reptiles fed on fish. If the plankton had died, so would the fish and so, perhaps, would all the fish-eating reptiles.

One suggestion is that small mammals which lived alongside the dinosaurs took to eating dinosaur eggs.

At first, mammals were not very numerous and ate relatively few eggs. Towards the end of the Cretaceous Period they became much more abundant and may have eaten so many eggs that dinosaurs died out.

Another suggestion is that the appearance of flowering plants, which often need insects to pollinate the flowers, encouraged a population explosion of butterflies and their larvae, caterpillars. The hungry caterpillars stripped all the plants bare, leaving nothing for the dinosaurs to eat. Without food, the dinosaurs thus died out.

"

Questions

1 A theory is a way of explaining why something happened.
  a List the theories about why the dinosaurs died out according to source **A**.
  b List the theories about why the dinosaurs died out according to source **B**.
  c Which theories are mentioned in both sources?
  d Why do they both mention this theory?

2 Do any of the theories make no sense? Explain why they don't make sense.

3 Source **A** mentions the explosion of a star. Source **B** mentions this as well. Do the sources agree about what happened after the explosion? Explain your answer.

4 Read source **A**. Can you find any evidence or proof in source **A** for any of the theories?

5 Source **B** says that radiation killed off the dinosaurs through the food chain
  a what is a food chain
  b does this food chain idea explain the death of all dinosaurs?

6 A fossil is the remains of a plant or animal that lived millions of years ago and has been turned to stone
  a how can fossils be helpful in telling us about the death of the dinosaurs?
  b why can't fossils tell us the main reason why dinosaurs died out.

7 What would we have to discover to prove that the theory about mammals eating dinosaur eggs was the main reason for the death of dinosaurs?

8 Some people would say that this chapter is not really history. Look at the other chapters in this section and explain how it is different from the others.

B From the 'Cartoon History of the Universe'.

Swing Riots

The word *comprehension* means understanding. The historian tries to understand or make sense of things left from the past.

Some of the things historians might use are shown on this page. When a historian looks at a document from the past he or she has some idea of what to look for and what to expect. When you look at these documents see if you can work out some of the questions the historian has to ask in order to understand the past.

The historian can only work things out after he or she knows what the documents mean.

See if you can work out what these documents say and how they might be used by a historian.

The documents are about the Swing Riots. These took place in rural areas of England during the 1820's and 1830's. One cause of them was that farm labourers were annoyed about the introduction of threshing machines onto farms. These machines took away their jobs. The labourers also felt that they were badly underpaid. Farmers and landowners took little notice of these complaints until the labourers took violent action.

'Captain Swing' was the name which the labourers used when they presented their demands to the landowners. Captain Swing was a mythical figure. He did not exist.

A Swing letter

> this is to inform you what you have to undergo Sentelmen if providing you Dont pull down your neschines and rise the poor mens wages the maried men give tow and six pence a day a day the singel tow shilings. or we will burn down your barns and you in them this is the last notis
> from W S

B Swing letter

> Sir
> Your name is down amongst the Black hearts in the Black Book and this is to advise you and the like of you, who are Parson Justasses, to make your wills Ye have been the Blackguard Enemies of the People on all occasions, Ye have not yet done as ye ought
> Swing

Questions

1. **a** Read source **A**. Some words are spelled incorrectly. List them. What do you think this tells you about the writer?
   b What is the writer of this letter complaining about?
   c What is the writer of this letter threatening to do?

2. Read document **B**
   Copy down three unusual words and say what is unusual about them.

3. Compare documents **A** and **B**.
   a Name two ways in which they are similar.
   b Name two ways in which they are different.

4. How else might we find out abut the Swing Rioters? Name two pieces of evidence and say what they might tell us.

5. How might each of these historians find 'Swing' letters and pictures useful and why?
   a 'local' historian: writing about a town or village.
   b 'national' historian: writing the history of Britain.
   c 'international' historian: writing a history of Europe.
   d biographer: writing the story of someone's life.

6. In the introduction we said that the historian has to ask some important questions about the evidence before he or she can make sense of it. Copy and complete the table, so as to explain how the questions might help the historian understand the document about the Swing Riots.
   The first one has been done for you.

Questions	How the questions might help us to understand documents **A** and **B**
a What sort of document is it?	It is a letter, so it is written to a person, who may be able to do something about the demands of the Swing Rioters.
b Who wrote or made the document?	
c Why was the document written or made?	
d When was the document written or made?	
e How might the person who received the letter have understood it?	

After Swing

After the Swing riots the government were interested in finding out about the condition of people living in the countryside, so they asked important local people a series of questions. One of them was about the recent riots. Here are the answers from parishes in Sussex.

Q53 Can you give the Commissioners any information respecting the causes and consequences of the agricultural Riots and Burnings of 1830 and 1831?

A ANGMERING John Cole Tomkins

" **Q53** Beer shops. "

B BRIGHTHELMSTONE George Chassereau, late Overseer (in charge of the poor)

" **Q53** Caused by wantonness, spleen or ill will, rather than from poverty and distress. "

C CHAILEY John Beard

" **Q53** From want of employment and frequenting of beer shops. "

D WEST CHILTINGTON William Bailee, Rector (clergyman)

" **Q53** Political agitation the Farmers screwing the poor too severely in their wages; they have now better wages.
I am of opinion that the Agricultural Labourers in general are not becoming convinced that the Gentry are their friends. "

E CHIDDINGLY Richard Lower, Vestry Clerk (helped run the church)

" **Q53** Low wages paid to men employed by the Parish. Our paupers were concerned in no riot because employed at 5 shillings per week. Paupers from other Parishes, who were kept in idleness at 5 shillings per week. "

F CRAWLEY James Newman, Overseer

" **Q53** No I cannot. I am happy to say in this neighbourhood we have had no burnings and very little rioting. "

G MOUNTFIELD Francis Hick, Overseer

" **Q53** Do not think it would have occurred in Sussex, but from the example of the Kentish Labourers. "

H PULBOROUGH John Austin, Clergyman

" **Q53** I decline answering this question any further than by saying the labourers were not the cause. "

I OLD SHOREHAM J. S. Turner, Overseer

" **Q53** Evil-disposed persons poisoned the minds of the labouring classes by their Lectures in various part of the Kingdom. "

These last sources are rather difficult. You will need a dictionary to help you, or you could go straight on to the questions now.

J WESTHAMPNETT Thomas Halsted

" **Q53** In some measure from the inflammatory part of the press, connected with the worst of all evils, the beer shops. "

K SOMPTING Thomas Turner

" **Q53** The low rate of wages given to the Agricultural Labourers. Many had been for some time out of employment, others engaged at such low wages that they could not bear up against their difficulties. This, with bad principles, diffused by inflammatory speeches and publications, produced a spirit of dis-

2: Working with Sources

M Title page of contemporary pamphlet

affection, which produced an attempt to redress their grievances, which they did to a certain extent by obtaining an increase of wages and more general employment. The fires arose principally from individual revenge.

L WEST DEAN John Woods

Q53 The minds of the working classes have been in a state of restlessness for many years, much more so than before the French Revolution, since which the circulation of various booklets, and beer house orators, have caused less deference and respect for their employers. A letter was circulated here in 1795, threatening landowners and farmers if they did not comply with certain regulations. Since that period high prices of corn, inadequacy of wages and the unhappy consequences of dependence on the Poor Rates have all tended to prepare their minds for change; and in the Agricultural Riots in 1830 many without distress joined in the cry, that a destruction of machinery would improve their condition. The principal uneasiness now proceeds from want of employment and from not obtaining enough. The general reliance on parish relief is the canker-worm which preys on the happiness, peace, and comfort both of the payers and receivers, and if not checked must lead to fresh disturbances and probably revolution.

Questions

1 a List the reasons the writers give for the agricultural riots.
  b How could you check to find out if these reasons were the cause of the riots?

2 a What sort of people are replying to the question about riots? List their jobs and anything else they had in common.
  b Who did the government *not* ask about the causes of the riots? Can you think of any reasons why not?

3 Compare the answers of John Cole Tomkins (**A**) with those of William Bailee (**D**). Is one more useful than the other for finding out about what caused the riots? Explain your answer.

4 Not all the answers from the whole of Sussex have been printed here.
  a Why have we missed some out?
  b How does this affect the page's usefulness as a source about the riots?

Transported to Australia

When Britain lost its American colonies in the 1780s the British authorities were faced with the problem of finding a new place to send or get rid of its unwanted criminals. Now that it was no longer possible to ship these 'undesirable' people to America, a new place had to be found.

In May 1787, 11 ships set sail from Portsmouth to Botany Bay, Australia, a place which had been charted by Captain Cook in 1770. In the following years many more 'convict' ships were sent to Australia. Who were the people who were transported to Australia and what crimes had they committed?

Source **A** gives us some important clues. It also provides us with a chance to work out a lot just by looking at the source carefully. Remember to look for the date when this source was produced and think about what it tells us about the way people understood the world in those days. You might well find some unusual differences with the way in which we see the world today!

A Sentences passed at Gloucester Assizes in the summer of 1825 ▶

Questions

1 Read Source **A**. Copy and complete this table.

Crimes for which death was recorded	Crimes punished by transportation	Crimes punished by imprisonment

2 Copy each of these statements and explain whether you think it is supported by the evidence in Source **A**. Give as much evidence as you can from Source **A** in your answer.
  a Stealing was always punished by imprisonment.
  b Crime was punished much more harshly in the 19th century than today.
  c Property was thought to be more important than the lives of poor people.
  d The most serious crimes were punished by transportation.

3 a Some of the punishments might seem strange or unfair to us today. Which ones? Why?
  b What is the problem of judging this source by today's standards?

AUGUST. 3rd 1826,

SENTENCES
Of all the Prisoners
TRIED AT
Glo'ster
ASSIZES.

Thos. James, for breaking open the house of John Nicholls, of St, James' Bristol, and stealing shirts, &c. — Death recorded.

Wm. James, for breaking open the house of John Cox, of St. Philip's, Bristol, and stealing 20 lbs weight of cheese — 7 Years Transp.

Arthur Britton, Samuel Crow, and Wm. Crow, for robbing Ann Hicks, on the highway, of 200 guineas in gold — Acquitted

Wm. Williams, for attempting to commit a rape on Hannah Roberts, an infant 10 years of age, at Littledean — 3 Years Imp.

George Gwilliam, for intent to commit a rape on Mary Gwilliam, of Stanton, against her will — 3 Years Imp.

James Jones, stealing a gelding from J. Calloway, Bristol — Death rec.

James Turner and Thos. Pegler, for robbing J. Underwood on the highway, of a hat — Death rec.

Wm. George, Thos. Parker, and Eliz. Parker, for house-breaking, at Old Sodbury, and stealing a bed quilt — 7 Years Transp.

Charles Bence, Henry John, Wm Hill, Doctnr Turner, for a riot, at Pyrton, and assalting several of his Majesty's subjects, particularly J. Coiter— pleaded Guilty: Entered into their own Recognizance,

Robert Hudson, for assaulting Jane Neale, at Stroud, with intent to commit a rape — Two Years Imp.

John Mico, and Robert Shackle, for stealing 2 sacks and 3 casks, from J. Staite, of Bristol — 7 Years Transp.

Richard Fowler, for stealing hay, at Winterbourne — 12 Months Imp.

John Cosburn, Sam. Watkins, and Richard Kirby, charged with killing and slaying John Richins — Acquitted

George Cooke, for housebreaking at Dursley, and stealing a tea caddy, & other articles — 7 Years Transp.

Charles Bessell, Marshall May, and Richard Groves, for breaking open the cellar of A Johnson, nt Baptist Mills, and stealing 2 dozen bottles of wine — Bessell and Groves, Death rec.; May, No Bill.

Sarah Mears, Sarah Orchard, Mary Ann Smith, Resolba Hopkins, and Ellen Wayland, for receiving the above wine, well knowing the same to have been stolen—Mears 14 Years Trans. Orchard, Smith & Wayland Acq. Hopkins, no bill

Geo. Goode, for killing T. Hawkins, at St. Briavel's — 18 months Imp.

Thos. Gardiner, for housebreaking at Chalford, steal. cloth — CONDEM.

Wm. Chivers, for breaking open the house of Fran. Cam, at Iron Acton, and stealing 21 cheeses — Transp. for Life.

Thos. Mills, and Wm. Mills, for breaking open the house of Wm. Cousins, at Wotton-Underedge, and stealing cloth—T. Mills, Evidence; Wm. Mills, CONDEMNED.

Hester James, Stephen Woodward, Job Mills, Wm. Dyer, John Dyer, Wm. Somers, and John S. Vines, for receiving the above cloth, knowing it to have been stolen— Woodward & James, Acq. the others ordered to remain.

Rich. Mee, for stealing a bottle of brandy at Cheltenham — 7 Years Tr.

Jas. Hayward, James Kerry, Fred. Clements, and Geo. King, for a burglary in the house of Fanny Newnuryi in Cneltenham, and stealing shoes, &c. Hayward, King's Evidence; Kerry & Clements, Acq. King, DEATH

John Farmer, for attempting to commit an uunatural crime on J. Chappell — Acquitted

Elizabeth Jones, for stealing calico, the property of W. Mumford; also for various other felonies, at Tewkesbury — Transp. for Life

Wm. Evans, and John Denner, for breaking open the cellar of A. Johnson, at Baptist Mills, and stealing 5 dozen bottles of wine — Death rec.

Isaiah John Langstreeth, for stealing tea, at Tewkesbury — 7 Yrs. Transp.

Aztecs

A An Aztec pyramid. The pyramid is a temple of the warriors, at Chichenitza in Mexico.

Sometimes we can't find out about certain things which happened in the past. There are many reasons for this.

One may be that there isn't any evidence. For example, the question 'how many oranges did Queen Victoria eat?' would be difficult to answer because we don't have the right sort of evidence. This may not be a surprise, because it might seem a rather silly question to ask. However there are many important questions which historians can't answer easily, because of the lack of evidence to help them. We might, for example, like to find out exactly what the Seven Wonders of the World looked like. We can't do this because most of them have been destroyed and weren't written about in detail at the time. Gaps make it harder to write history books because we cannot find out about certain people, places or events which we think are important.

Sometimes there are particulary important reasons for the gaps. Documents may have been lost. Sometimes nothing was written or produced anyway. On other occasions one side of the story has not been told. For example the Bayeux Tapestry only tells the Norman side of the story of the Conquest of England in 1066. It ignores the Saxon point of view and leaves out things the Saxons might be proud of — such as King Harold's victory over the Vikings at the Battle of Stamford Bridge.

So we need to look at evidence carefully. We need to be aware of what the evidence does and does not tell us. Often a document is more interesting for what it doesn't say than for what it does say. The following exercise contains material, most of it from one point of view, but this doesn't mean that it is useless to us.

The documents are about the Aztecs of Mexico. Most of these documents were written or made under the direction of the Spaniards after they had conquered the Aztec empire in the 1520's. They describe what seemed to the Spanish as the barbaric practice of human sacrifice and cannibalism. This showed a particularly brutal and unpleasant side to Aztec civilisation. The Aztecs weren't allowed to explain why they did these things.

Look at the documents and see what sense later historians have made of the Spanish evidence about the Aztecs. The documents are about the Aztecs, but you should also be able to work out things about the Spaniards. They also tell us something about the ways historians make use of the evidence.

C Spanish eyewitness description of Aztec sacrifice from Bernal Diaz's 'History of New Spain'

Bernal Diaz was a soldier and adventurer who was with Cortes during the conquest of the Aztec Empire. Forty years after the campaign, when he was seventy, he wrote a detailed account of what he had seen. This document was originally written in Spanish.

"

'We saw them put plumes on the heads of many of them, and then they made them dance with a sort of fan in front of Huitzilopochtli. Then, after they had danced, the priests laid them on their backs on some narrow stones of sacrifice and, cutting open their chests, drew out their palpitating hearts which they offered to the idols before them. Then they kicked the bodies down the steps, and the Indian butchers who were waiting below cut off their arms and legs and flayed their faces, which they afterwards prepared like glove leather, with their beards on, and kept for their drunken festivals. Then they ate their flesh with a sauce of peppers and tomatoes.'

"

B A scene from a Mexican 'Codex' showing human sacrifice. This picture was taken from a Codex made in 1553. It gives us an account in pictures of Aztec life. Codexes were usually produced by local artists working under Spanish direction. The Aztecs didn't have a written language.

The Aztecs

D William Hickling Prescott was an American historian who spent most of his life researching into the history of the Aztecs and Incas.

> 'Human sacrifice however cruel, has nothing in it degrading to its victim. It may be rather said to ennoble him, by devoting him to the gods. Although so terrible with the Aztecs, it was sometimes voluntarily embraced by them, as the most glorious death, and one that opened a sure passage into paradise. The Inquisition[1], on the other hand, branded its victims with infamy[2] in this world, and consigned them to everlasting perdition[3] in the next.
>
> One detestable feature of the Aztec superstition, however, sunk it far below the Christian. This was its cannibalism; though, in truth, the Mexicans were not cannibals, in the coarsest acceptation of the term. They did not feed on human flesh merely to gratify a brutish appetite, but in obedience to their religion. Their repasts[4] were made of the victims whose blood had been poured out on the altar of sacrifice. This is a distinction worthy of notice. Still, cannibalism, under any form, or whatever sanction[5], cannot but have a fatal influence on the nation addicted to it. It suggests ideas so loathsome, so degrading to man, to his spirtual and immortal nature, that it is impossible the people who practise it should make any great progress in moral or intellectual culture.'

[1]Disciplining of free thinking Catholics; [2]ill fame; [3]damnation; [4]meals; [5]legal authorization; [6]simple or boring; [7]people who study the behaviour of people; [8]shortage; [9]add to; [10]government controlled

E An account of why Aztecs were cannibals

This extract comes from an English school history book called the 'Clash of Cultures', published in 1981 by Heinemann Educational Books. It was written by a history lecturer, Brian Catchpole.

> 'A much more mundane[6] explanation for the persistent sacrifice of prisoners of war and slaves can be found in the writings of anthropologists[7] Michael Harner and Marvyn Harris. They argue that the absence of cattle, sheep, goats, and horses (in itself an explanation of why the Aztec culture rejected the wheel as a basis of transport — there were no beasts of burden) meant a deficiency[8] of animal protein in Aztec diet. Turkeys and dogs were abundant in Mexico and theoretically might have helped to meet this deficiency. But turkeys fed on grain and Aztecs couldn't afford to domesticate them in quantity; and dogs were essential as the basic scavengers of Aztec life.
>
> So, if the Chief of Men could ensure that religious rituals (when literally thousands of people might be sacrificed) coincided with food shortages, the cannibalism was not simply ceremonial. Montezuma and his predecessors ensured that there were regular supplies of human flesh to supplement[9] the basically vegetarian diet — or even replace it in times of famine. Marvyn Harris does not hesitate to describe Aztec priests as "ritual slaughterers in a state-sponsored[10] system geared to the production and redistribution of substantial amounts of animal protein in the form of human flesh."'

Questions

1. Looking at picture **A** what can you work out about the people who built the temple?

2. What similarities are there between picture **B** and evidence **C**?

3. **a** Read evidence **D** and **E**. What do they disagree about?
   b Why might they disagree?

4. Would the Aztecs have been able to give either of the reasons in evidence **D** or **E** for their cannibalism? Explain your answer.

5. Why might the Spanish have wanted to show the Aztecs as brutal and unpleasant?

6. Suggest some reasons why the Aztecs didn't write history books about the Spanish Invasion.

7. Much of the information on this page only presents the Spanish point of view about the conquest of the Aztec Empire. How might this affect our attitude towards
   a the Aztecs,
   b the Spanish?

The Battle of Isandhlwana

In the year 1879 the British army invaded Zululand in what is now known as South Africa. The British army was beaten by the Zulus at the Battle of Isandhlwana. This defeat was an unusual happening, because the British army did not lose many battles against African peoples in the nineteenth century.

Look through the sources of evidence on this and the next pages to find clues about why the British lost the battle. Remember to look at the sources together, because one source sometimes only tells you part of what you want to discover.

A Eye-witness account of the battle of Isandhlwana by Lieutenant Horace Dorien-Smith, from a letter in the Brecon County Times, 29 March 1879

"

When I arrived in camp, I found the greater part of the column gone out with the General to meet the Zulu force.... The first Zulu force appeared about six o'clock in the morning. Two companies of the 24th were sent out after them. The Zulus seemed to retire.... At about ten thirty the Zulus were seen coming over the hills in thousands. They were in most perfect order. They were in a semi-circle round our two flanks and in front of us and must have covered several miles of ground. Nobody knows how many there were of them, but the general idea is at least 20,000.

Well, to cut the account short, in half an hour they were right up to the camp.... Bullets were flying all over the place, but I never seemed to notice them. The Zulus nearly all had firearms ... and lots of ammunition.... On looking round we saw that we were completely surrounded and the road to Rorke's Drift was cut off. The place where they seemed thinnest was where we all made for. Everybody went pellmell over ground covered with high boulders and rocks until we got to a deep ... gully. We had to go bang through them ... lots of our men were killed there. I had lots of marvellous escapes, and was firing away at them with my revolver as I galloped along.... This lasted till we came to a kind of precipice down to the river Buffalo.

I jumped off and led my horse down.

The horse went with a bound to the bottom of the precipice, being struck with an assegai ... the Zulus were all around me.... I rushed off on foot and plunged into the river, which was little better than a roaring torrent.

I was being carried down stream at a tremendous pace, when a loose horse came by me and I got hold of his tail and he landed me safely on the other bank....

About twenty Zulus got over the water and followed us up the hill....

Well, to cut it short, I struggled into Helpmakaar, about twenty miles off ... to find a few men who had escaped.

"

B Eye-witness account of the battle of Isandhlwana by Private Patrick Farrell, from a letter in the South Wales Daily Telegram, 27 March 1879

"

... Dear brother, when the column got well out from camp, Zulus came on the camp and took away everything there; killed sixteen officers and five companies of the 1/24th, five officers and 179 of the 2/24th....

About six o'clock we came back towards camp, and it was dark, so we had to take the camp ground at any price, but the rascals fled ... so we slept that night amongst dead bodies (black and white) ... and in the morning, to look at the camp; what a state! 1,000 white men, and 5,000 black men killed! waggons broke! bullocks killed! tents all gone! It was the most horrid sight that was ever seen by a soldier, dear brother.... Worst than ever was done in the Indian Mutiny.... All the boys from Tredegar are safe....

"

C Eye-witness account of the battle of Isandhlwana by Lieutenant W. Cochrane, from the Hereford Times, 29 March 1879

"

... The Zulus appeared in force in front of us and to our left. They were in skirmishing order but ten or twelve deep, with supports close behind. They opened fire at us about 800 yards, and advanced rapidly. We retired steadily in skirmishing order ... when we came upon the remains of the Rocket battery, which had been cut off and broken up; there was a hand-to-hand engagement going on with those that remained....

A few mounted men and a great many natives managed to escape from the camp, but had to ride hard over very rough country to the Buffalo River ... under fire from the enemy the whole way. The ground was so bad for horses that the Zulus on foot were able to run as fast as the horses could travel. I should judge that more than half the number that left the camp were killed before they arrived at the Buffalo, and many more were drowned, there being no drift, the water running rapidly.... The fighting lasted from about eleven thirty a.m. till one p.m.... There must have been at least 15,000 Zulus, beside the reserves, and I should compute the numbers killed at from 2,000 to 2,500. The Zulu system of attack . . . is easily traceable, the main body being opposite the left centre of the camp; the horns thrown out to the left rear and right front. Had the Zulus completed their scheme, by sending a column to the Buffalo River to cut off the retreat, not a man would have escaped to tell the tale.

"

D A Zulu warrior remembers the battle of Isandhlwana, quoted in 'A sketch of the Kaffir and Zulu Wars' by Captain H Hallam-Parr of the British army

"

Ah those red soldiers at Isandhlwana. How few they were and how they fought! They fell like stones — each man in his place.

"

E A drawing from the Illustrated London News, showing the British cavalry revisiting the field of the battle of Isandhlwana to bring away the wagons after the battle (published in 1879)

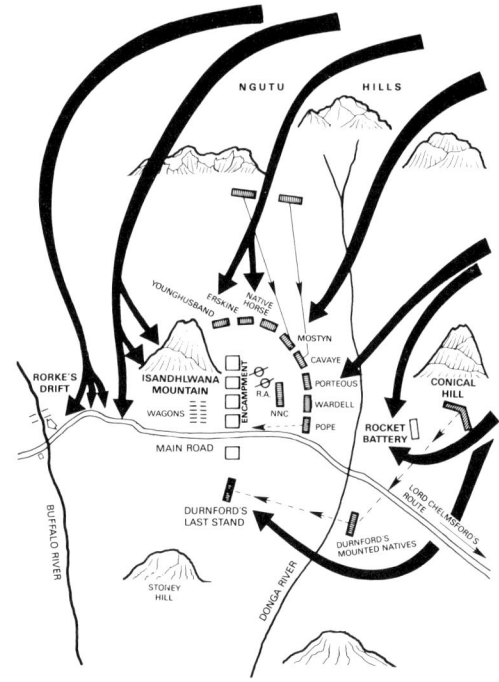

F Map of the battle of Isandhlwana, 22 January 1879 (from 'The Scramble for Africa' by Robin Brooke-Smith, Macmillan, 1987)

2: Working with Sources

G Reinforcements searching for English dead on the battlefield of Isandhlwana, shortly after the battle

H Table showing strength of British army columns at the battle of Isandhlwana

CASUALTIES DURING THE CAMPAIGN

Action	Engaged		Killed		Wounded		Remarks
	Officers	NCOs and Men	Officers	NCOs and Men	Officers	NCOs and Men	
Isandhlwana	67	1,707	52	806	–	–	471 natives also killed

Questions

1. According to sources **A** and **C**:
   a How many Zulus were at Isandhlwana?
   b Why might the sources disagree?
2. How did the British soldiers behave in the battle? Support your answer with quotations from sources **A** and **D**.
   b Why might Source **D** give a different answer from Source **A**?
3. Compare Sources **B** and **H**. Do they agree or disagree about the number of people who were killed in the battle? Support your answer with quotations from the sources.
4. Sources **E** and **G** show the site of Isandhlwana after the battle.
   a What similarities do you notice?
   b Why are they different?
5. Sources **A**, **B** and **C** are eye-witness accounts of the battlefield. In what ways are eye-witness accounts: a reliable; b unreliable as evidence of the battle of Isandhlwana?
   Explain your answers.
6. The story of the battle of Isandhlwana is told by white people or through white people on the British side in the war. How does this affect our understanding of the Zulus?
7. Why can we not be certain about the number of Zulu casualties in the war?
8. Look at the map, Source **F**.
   How do you think the person who drew the map worked out the positions of the soldiers?

Was Hitler Mad?

More books have been written about Hitler, the leader of Nazi Germany, than any other person, but how much do we really know about him? What sort of person was he?

In this exercise you are going to look at different sorts of evidence about Hitler, and then try to examine the statement that has sometimes been made about him: that he was a madman.

Do these sources prove that he was mad? Think about the sort of evidence you might need to back up such an opinion.

A Cartoon 'Jekyll and Hyde' about Hitler, by the British cartoonist, Bernard Partridge, 17th April, 1940, in 'Punch' magazine

B Official photograph of Hitler taken as he looked out from an aeroplane in March 1938 onto his Austrian homeland (Hitler's Germany was joined up with German-speaking Austria in March 1938. This was something Hitler had wanted to do for a long time.)

C Unofficial photograph of Hitler taken whilst he was leader of Germany

D Public speech by Hitler, 5th February 1928

"The idea of struggle is as old as life itself, for life is only preserved because other living things perish through struggle. In this struggle, the stronger, the more able, win, while the less able, the weak, lose. Struggle is the father of all things. It is not by the principles of humanity that man lives or is able to preserve himself above the animal world, but solely by means of the most brutal struggle."

E Statement by a French soldier to the Czech historian, J.P. Stern, in 1940

"I admire your Führer.
I must admire him because he has done everything that he promised himself he would do."

F From 'The History of Germany since 1789' by the German historian, Golo Mann, 1974

"Hitler lived by a few simple ideas: Nature is cruel. As part of nature man is justified in being cruel. Life is war. There is always war, only its form changes. As a predatory animal lives at the expense of other animals a nation lives at the expense of other nations. What it wants to enjoy it must take away from others. If it wants to enjoy safety it must exterminate its neighbours...

Compassion, charity, truthfulness, loyalty to obligations, all the Christian virtues are inventions of cowards and weaklings. Nature does not know them; the strong man does not observe them. He kills the weak; he lies and breaks treaties where it is to his advantage. The world has always been like this, all great empires have risen in this way, the Roman, the British, and the German Empire too shall arise in this way..."

G From 'Hitler, The Fuehrer and the People' by the Czech historian J.P. Stern, (Fontana 1975). As a boy in Prague in March 1939 Stern watched Hitler's troops march into the Czech capital. He also heard some of Hitler's speeches. He later fought in the Royal Air Force against the Nazis.

"A colleague, a professor from Munich University, at Hitler's trial in February 1924, describes him in the language characteristic of the age, the language which Hitler made his own: 'For the first time I saw Hitler at close quarters. Face and head: bad race, mongrel. Low, receding forehead, ugly nose, broad cheekbones, small eyes, dark hair. Facial expression: not of a man commanding with full self-control, but betraying insane excitement. Finally, an expression of blissful egotism.'"

H Description of Hitler by a British diplomat who met him in the 1930's when Hitler was leader of Germany (before Britain was at war with Germany).

"Hitler himself look well and young. He is not like his ordinary photographs or the impression given of him abroad. He does not look like either a fanatic[1] or a poseur[2]. He does not make a disagreeable impression. He is simple and direct — a man of the people, with no claim to the prophet's mantle or the emperor's crown.

His speech was clear and easily intelligible. There appeared to be no oratorical or emotional tricks. The emotion came from the crowd..."

[1] Person filled with excessive enthusiasm for an idea; [2] Person who tries to make an effect.

I Description of Hitler by David Lloyd George, who had just returned from a visit to Hitler in 1935, (Lloyd George had been Liberal Prime Minister of Britain during and shortly after World War I.)

> He is a born leader of men. A magnetic, dynamic personality with a single-minded purpose. He is not merely in name, but in fact the natural leader. He has made them safe against potential enemies by whom they are surrounded. The old trust him. The young idolize him...

J Speech by Adolf Hitler to a secret meeting of his army commanders, 22nd August 1939, just before the start of World War II

> I shall give a propagandist reason for starting the war, no matter whether it is plausible; or not. The victor will not be asked afterwards whether he told the truth or not. When starting and waging war it is not right that matters, but victory.
>
> Close your hearts to pity. Act brutally. Eighty million people must obtain what is their right. Their existence must be made secure. The strongest man is right.

K From 'A History of Germany' by the British historian William Carr, 1969

> Hitler's personality was unattractive in the extreme. He was a changeable and moody individual, excessively vain, full of overweening pride and ambition, not without intellectual ability but shallow and superficial in his judgements and firmly convinced of his own infallibility[1] over the whole range of human experience. At bottom Hitler was a profoundly lonely and isolated human being, deeply contemptuous of mankind in general, inordinately[2] suspicious of his fellow men, unscrupulous[3], brutal and utterly ruthless in his methods and totally lacking in human compassion. From his earliest days he suffered from deep-seated emotional instability; a pathological liar, he was for ever on the verge of tears, lurching easily from rational discussion into uncontrollable hysterical outbursts. But his political gifts were of the very highest order. He possessed tremendous energy and remarkable will-power and in his quest for high office displayed the single-mindedness of a fanatic. The supreme opportunist[4] completely cynical[5] in his contempt for principles — not excluding those on which his own party was supposedly based — he had an uncanny sense of timing and an unerring instinct for the course of action most likely to advance his interests.

L From 'The War Path' by David Irving, 1978

> The post-war world's view of (Hitler) has been so conditioned by our own propaganda against him, that only the cartoon caricature of him prevails; hence any account based on authentic records of the era is bound to enhance history's view of him in some respects — although it will detract from it in many others. I have tried to accord him the kind of hearing that he would have got in an English court of law — where the normal rules of evidence apply, but also where a measure of insight is appropriate.

[1]**Inability to be mistaken or make a mistake;** [2]**Excessively;** [3]**Shameless;** [4]**Person who grasps any opportunity;** [5]**Doubting other's sincerity.**

Questions

1 First we need to sort out these sources. Make a list of the different types of source in this section. The list is started for you.
   political cartoon
   photograph

2 Source **A** shows Hitler becoming mad. According to the cartoon, what makes him change?

3 Compare Sources **A** and **H**.
   In what ways do they disagree about Hitler? Support your explanation with quotations from both sources.

4 Compare Sources **D** and **F**.
   In what ways do they agree about Hitler's ideas? Support your explanation with quotations from both sources.

5 Compare Sources **D** and **J**.
   a Had Hitler changed his ideas in the 11 years between these sources?
      Explain your answer.
   b Source **D** is a public speech by Hitler, Source **J** is a private speech to army commanders.
      Is it important for an historian to know if a source is 'public' or 'private'? Give reasons.

6 Source **D** is a primary source about Hitler's ideas. Source **K** is a secondary source.
   Are secondary sources less reliable about Hitler's ideas, or can they tell us things primary sources cannot?

7 a What differences do you notice in the way in which Hitler is shown in the cartoon (Source **A**) and in photograph **C**?
   b 'The cartoon must be less reliable than either of the photographs as evidence of Hitler's personality, because it must be less accurate.'
      Do you agree? Explain your answer.

8 This question is worth lots of marks, so try and plan your answer carefully. Try to include evidence from as many of the sources as you can.
   'Hitler was mad.' Do these sources show this statement to be true? Explain your answer in long paragraphs.

'Bloody Sunday'

Background information

On Sunday 30th January 1972 in Londonderry, Civil Rights groups decided that they would hold a march to protest against internment[1]. The government had made such marches illegal. Rather than ban the march, the government had used the army which included the 1st Parachute Regiment (1 Para.) to keep the marchers within the Catholic Bogside area of Londonderry. By the end of the day 13 civilians were dead. The event came to be known as 'Bloody Sunday'.

After Bloody Sunday there were two inquiries into the event. One, the Widgery Report, was the official British inquiry; the other, the Dash Report, was organised by the National Council for Civil Liberties.

[1] Confining of suspects without trial.

A Photograph taken on Sunday 30th January 1972 in Londonderry

'Bloody Sunday'

B Father Bradley, a Catholic priest

"It was a massacre. I saw no one shooting at troops. If anybody had been, I would have seen it. I saw only the Army shooting. The British Army should hang its head in shame after today's disgusting violence. They shot indiscriminately and everywhere around them without any provocation. I was administering the last rites to a boy about fifteen who had been shot by soldiers in Rossville Street. While I was there I saw three other people who had been shot down in the middle of the street. Two of them have since died, one a young boy. It was impossible to get out to them; they were lying behind the barricade. I could only get about ten yards towards them, so I administered the last rites from there. Then the paratroops arrived. I think there may have been up to twenty of them, and they pushed about ten of us up against the wall of the courtyard. We couldn't move one way or another. One paratrooper beside me aimed at least eight shots indiscriminately at a group of people that were fleeing. I grabbed him and shouted; 'For God's sake, stop!' He just shrugged me off. What really frightened me was that some of them seemed to enjoy it. I heard some of them making crude jokes as people were falling. God Almighty — it's only really now getting home to me!"

C Lt-Colonel Derek Wilford, in charge of 1 Para

"It's unfortunate but when we got up there past William Street, here, where we're standing, and up towards Rossville Flats, we came under fire. We came under fire from the bottom of the Flats, from the Flats; we were also petrol-bombed, and some acid, in fact, was poured on us from the top of the Flats.

When we're fired at, we must protect ourselves."

D Extract from the Dash Report

"A large-scale arrest operation by the paratroopers was unjustified. The main body of the marchers had accepted the military action to contain the march in the Bogside area and had avoided any confrontation with the military or police forces. Although a hooligan group had thrown an assortment of missiles, none of which were explosive . . . the soldiers were successful in dispersing these rioters by the use of rubber bullets, CS gas, and a high-pressure water cannon. Photographs had been taken by the Army, and arrests of the rioters could have been made later, at a time which would not endanger the large number of peaceable civilians who were in the Bogside . . . because of the march."

E Extract from the Widgery Report

"If the Army had persisted in its 'low key' attitude and had not launched a large-scale operation to arrest hooligans, the day might have passed off without serious incident.

There was no general breakdown in Army discipline . . . soldiers who identified armed gunmen fired upon them in accordance with the standing orders in the Yellow Card. Each soldier was his own judge of whether he had identified a gunman . . . At one end of the scale, some soldiers showed a high degree of responsibility, at the other . . . firing bordered on the reckless."

Questions

1. Read Source **B**. Father Bradley described the event as a 'massacre'. How does he back up this view of the event? Support your answer by quoting from Source **B**.

2. Read Source **C**. Lieutenant-Colonel Derek Wilford said of the event, 'When we're fired at, we must protect ourselves.' How does he back up this view of the event? Support your answer by quoting from Source **C**.

3. **a** Father Bradley said the event was a 'massacre'. Is this a fact or an opinion? Explain your answer.
   b How could we check if Father Bradley's description of the event as a 'massacre' is accurate?

4. In the photograph (**A**) the marchers appear to be peaceful. Does this mean that the march was always peaceful? Explain your answer.

5. Read the two reports of the events of the day (source **D** and **E**). How are they different in their views about:
   a what the army did on the day;
   b what the civilian marchers did on the day.

6. The sources provide us with different points of view about what happened on 'Bloody Sunday'. Does this mean that some of the sources are useless? Explain your answer carefully.

Gleaners

A Photograph of two gleaners

B From 'Tess of the d'Urbevilles' by Thomas Hardy

He was a writer who lived in Dorset at the beginning of the twentieth century, and wrote novels set in the countryside.
Hardy describes how Tess and her friend Marian spend the day hoeing in a swede field.

"
They worked on hour after hour, unconscious of the forlorn aspect they bore in the landscape, not thinking of the justice or injustice of their lot ... In the afternoon the rain came on again ... It was so high a situation, this field that the rain had no occasion to fall, but raced along horizontally upon the yelling wind, sticking into them like glass splinters till they were wet through. Tess had not known till now what was really meant by that. There are degrees of dampness, and a very little is called being wet through in common talk. But to stand working slowly in a field, and feel the creep of rainwater, first in legs and shoulders, then on hips and head, then at back, front, and sides, and yet to work on till the leaden light diminishes and marks that the sun is down, demands a distinct modicum of stoicism, even of valour.
"

C From 'Toilers of the Field', by Richard Jeffries

He was an English writer and journalist and wrote a lot about the countryside.

"
Does the incessant labour undergone by an agricultural woman result in ill effects to her physical frame? The day-work in the fields, the haymaking, and such labour as is paid for by the day and not by the piece, cannot do any injury, for it is light, and the hours are short. In some districts the women do not come in before half-past eight, and leave a little after four, and they have a long hour out for dinner.
"

D The opinions of Richard Jeffries quoted in a book by Rafael Samuel, a modern historian who has written books about poor people in the countryside.

"
The field labouring girl was held to be spoiled alike for domestic service and for marriage, 'coarsened' by her work — and by the mixed company she kept — to the point that womanliness was destroyed.
"

2: Working with Sources

E 'Les Glaneuses' (Gleaners), a painting by J. F. Millet, 1857

Questions

1 Look at sources **E** and **F**.
   a What similarities do you notice? Mention things you see in both pictures.
   b What differences do you notice?
   c Why might they be different?

2 Look at source **A**. Is it more like source **E** or source **F**? Give reasons for your answer.

3 Source **A** is a photograph. Does that mean it must be more reliable than the painting shown in source **E** as evidence about the lives of gleaners?

4 Source **F** is not about gleaners. Does that mean it is of no value as evidence about the lives of working people in the countryside?

5 How reliable is source **B** as evidence about the lives of working women? Comment on these two problems:
   a Source **B** was written about 80 years after the events it describes:
   b Source **B** is a novel.

6 According to Jeffries (source **C**) how hard was women's work? Quote from source **C** to support your answer.

Gleaners

F 'The Hireling Shepherd', a painting by Holman Hunt

Questions

7 Use evidence from sources **A** and **E** to explain what you think gleaning was.

8 All these sources were made or written by men. Does that mean they are unreliable as evidence of the lives of working women?

9 Source **D** gives a different impression of how hard women's work was from that given in source **C**. What is the difference?

10 Richard Jeffries wrote source **C** and his opinions are mentioned in source **D**. Can you suggest any reasons why he seems to say different things in the two sources?

11 a Name two other sources you might use to find out more about gleaners.
   b What would you hope to find out from each of these sources?

Asking Questions

In this final section we want to go over a few points that were made in the introduction and suggest other ways of looking at evidence. We will also go over some of the things that you have learnt.

To answer these questions you will need to be sure that you understand the work that we have introduced you to in this book. Answer these questions using examples that you can find from anywhere in the book. (Copy each title and write your answer to the question below it.)

Primary and Secondary Sources
On page 14 we mentioned the difference between primary and secondary sources. Now find two examples of primary sources and two examples of secondary sources to do with wars. Explain how a historian interested in the effects of war on people could use them.

Similarities and Differences
On page 12 about the bombing of Coventry we found that there were two different accounts of the same event. Now look through the book and find any two other examples of different accounts of the same event or story.

Facts and Opinion
In the story of the bombing of Coventry page 14 there is a question asking you about Facts and Opinions. Find another piece of evidence that contains opinions as well as facts. Copy out bits from it and explain your answer.

Points of View
We saw on page 48 that people in the past had different opinions about the same thing. This is just as true today. Find a piece of evidence from which different groups of people might be able to draw different conclusions.

Why was it written or made?
It's important to know why something was made. For example, a portrait is usually painted to show what the person looks like, or sometimes to flatter them. A cartoon usually exaggerates a person's features or characteristics.
   Choose a source from anywhere in the book and try to explain *why* it was made.

Asking Questions

A Representatives of Soviet, British and American Governments at a debate in the United Nations.

What is it?
Here is a photograph we looked at earlier. On page 19 we saw how the photo could be understood differently. We need to know the background to the event to understand the photograph properly.

Choose any photograph in the book and explain what it appears to show and in what ways it is useful as a piece of evidence. Then write down what else you need to know about the photograph before you can make your mind up about how reliable it is.

Testing Ideas

If you managed to complete the previous section about asking questions, then you should be able to have a go at understanding and answering this section.

Read these statement, copy each of them out and explain if you agree or disagree with it. Use evidence from the book to help you. Try a section at a time.

A

- A primary source must always be more reliable than a secondary source.
- A photograph is more useful than a painting.
- A secondary source is more useful than a primary source.
- An eye witness account must be reliable.

B

- If two sources say different things then one of them must be lying.
- You can understand why sources say different things if you know who wrote the source and why.
- The same piece of evidence can be both reliable and unreliable.
- The same piece of evidence can be understood in different ways.

C

- A piece of evidence that just gives us one point of view is unreliable.
- There are *two* sides to every story.
- Evidence only becomes evidence when it is useful for something.
- Sources become reliable or unreliable depending on the questions you ask them.
- When we describe as a source of evidence it suggests that we have the solution to a particular question.

Where do we go from here?

In this book we have not been looking for 'right' or 'wrong' answers. We have just been interested in the different way that people understand evidence from the past.

History is not just one long story that should be learnt, it is about arguments, points of view and trying to prove your case. Sometimes the evidence for one point of view is convincing, sometimes it isn't. It often depends on your age, or the country where you live. The past in other words is presented to us by historians who are influenced by just the same kind of things.

To make sense of history we need to know about the person that wrote the book. History books are sources of evidence just like anything else and so we must ask of them the same questions that we would about any other piece of evidence.

Index

A
Armada 8–9, 10
Australia 38
Aztecs 40–42

B
Bayeux Tapestry 24–25, 40
Bloody Sunday, 1972 51–53

C
cartoons 25, 50, 57
child labour 10–11
children 10–11, 30–31
codex 41
Columbus, Christopher 26–29
Coventry 12–13, 14, 15, 57

D
Dash Report 51–52
diaries 14
dinosaurs 32–33
documents 21, 26, 31, 34, 35, 40

E
eye-witness accounts 43, 45, 60

F
factory conditions 10–11

G
gleaners 54–56

H
history books 4, 17, 26, 42
Hitler, Adolf 46–50

I
Isandhlwana 43–45

L
letters 20, 30–31, 34, 43
Londonderry 51–52

N
Nazi Germany 46
Northern Ireland 51–53

O
Oral History 16–17

P
paintings 22–23, 55, 56, 57, 60
photographs 13, 14–17, 18–19, 21, 45, 46, 50, 55, 58, 60
photojournalism 18
Picture Post 17
primary sources 14, 20, 50, 57, 60

R
rock painting 22–23

S
secondary sources 14, 50, 57, 60
South Africa 43
Swing Riots 34–35, 36–37

T
textbooks 8, 9, 26, 29, 60
theory 32
transportation 38–39

W
war 12–15, 20–21, 30–31, 43–45
Widgery Report 51–52
World War II 30–31

Acknowledgements

The authors and publishers would like to thank the following organisations for help with illustrations in this book:

National Maritime Museum, London (8); Mansell Collection (10); Popperfoto (12,15,51); Hulton Picture Company (17,54); Associated Press (18-19,59); Robert Harding (16-17); Geopics (17); The Widening World: A Jean Landesborough M.A. © George Philip & Son Ltd 1954 (26); Ladybird Books Ltd, Loughborough for material (27-28) from *Christopher Columbus* by L Du Garde Peach; © Larry Gorrick (All rights reserved) (33); Pat Morris (40); John R Freeman and Co (Photographers) Ltd (41); Illustrated London News (44); Royal Commonwealth Society (45); David Irving Collection (46); Punch (47); Cliché des Musées Nationaux Paris (55); City of Manchester Art Gallery (56).

They would also like to thank the following for help with text:

Historical Associated for *English History to Foreign Eyes* by J Hunt; Ladybird Books Ltd, Loughborough for extracts from *Christopher Columbus* by L Du Garde Peach; The Tom Harrisson Mass Observation Archive for excerpts from *Children at War*, published by the University of Sussex; extract from *Usborne Spotter's Guide: Dinosaurs* by D Norman published by Usborne Publishing Ltd; Heinemann Educational Books for extract from *Clash of Cultures* by Brian Catchpole; Penguin Books for the extract from Bernal Diaz: *The Conquest of New Spain*, translated by J M Cohen (Penguin Classics 1983) © J M Cohen 1963.